Trinity

COUNTING THEM IN
the inclusion of isolated bilingual learners

COUNTING THEM IN
the inclusion of isolated bilingual learners

edited by Liz Statham

Trentham Books

Stoke on Trent, UK and Sterling, USA

Trentham Books Limited
Westview House   22883 Quicksilver Drive
734 London Road   Sterling
Oakhill   VA 20166-2012
Stoke on Trent   USA
Staffordshire
England ST4 5NP

First published 2008

British Library Cataloguing-in-Publication Data
A catalogue record for this book is available from the British Library

ISBN: 978 1 85856 425 8

Cover illustration: Martin Reid. The Media Workshop – Southampton.
www.mpmw.co.uk

Designed and typeset by Trentham Print Design Ltd, Chester and
printed in Great Britain by Cromwell Press Limited, Trowbridge.

Contents

Dedication

This book is dedicated to a bilingual learner who arrived in Hampshire aged ten, the only bilingual learner in her primary school and the only Mandarin speaker in her secondary school. Abandoned by her parents in her teenage years, possibly because she has an older brother and was born in a country with a one child policy, she has gone on to take a degree in economics and produce a Chinese Society fashion show in aid of the Tsunami victims. She is aiming to be a lawyer.

Thanks

Many thanks to everyone who contributed, often from a distance – not a surprise in an isolated area! Many thanks to the core writing group of contributors plus Luci Woodland, the vignette writers – Lyn Adams, Eleri Bailey, Philippa Richmond and Julian Raley and the ex-isolated bilingual learners – Gurmit, Harish and Gus. Many thanks to the rest of the Hampshire Ethnic Minority Achievement Service who tholed the book's delivery. Particular thanks go to Stacey Oszczyk for brilliant technical back-up.

Preface

The following three pieces show what it was like for isolated bilingual learners to achieve success in the UK. As adults they have kindly agreed to reflect on their childhood experiences.

Gurmit

I was seven years old when we arrived in the United Kingdom. My father came here two years before us. I could not speak or understand a word of English. I remember going to the infant school and sitting there looking around and getting frustrated. Other children used to laugh at me and bully me in the playground. I didn't know how to complain and started to respond by kicking and pushing them. After a couple of months I started to understand the playground language but still found it very hard to cope with the class-work. At the end of junior school I still could not read or spell even basic words. After school I stayed at home most of the time as I was scared to go out. Mum and Dad didn't know anything, they worked long hours and I didn't want to worry them. I felt like I was a failure.

When I went to comprehensive school, there was a special class held for children who needed more help; it mainly consisted of children with behavioural problems. The teacher was always late so we spent most of the time messing around. By this time my only interest was football. After school hours and during the weekends I spent most of the time playing football. I was labelled as a bully in school. Lots of children were scared of me. I left school with two CSEs in Art and Geography. I could read and write basic simple sentences.

When I left school I got into bad company. One day, one of my friends was caught stealing in a shop and he involved me in it as I was with him. I got really scared and that was the turning point for me. I went to college and studied engineering for a year and got a part-time job as a trainee tool maker. All of my cousins did really well in schools and colleges and went to universities. When we all got together I felt I had nothing to talk about and felt really down. I had a feeling their parents didn't want them to mix with me as I was not a good role model. After about two years, I left my job and started helping my father who used to sell women's clothes in markets in different towns. I really enjoyed doing the markets. We bought two shops and the business was running really well. I was always interested in cars so I started buying car magazines and newspapers to keep up with the prices. This is how I learnt to read.

Suddenly, during the recession time in 1985, we had a great loss in business and lost both shops and even our house. My father and mother got jobs in factories and I carried on running the markets. Then I started with one car and since then I haven't looked back. I have been in the car business for twenty years. I think I have achieved more than I ever thought I would and feel very proud of myself.

Harish

I started at a primary school on my sixth birthday. It was at a state run school in the centre of Nairobi. I spent seven years there, and from the age of eight when we were first graded or ranked, I was top of my class. However, we were aware that there were other, expensive, private schools which were therefore likely to be better. The subtext was that being top of the class in this school would mean little in the context of the overall age group if all schools were considered. It was certainly the case that very few pupils from that school gained admission to the top secondary schools in Nairobi. The academic requirements for entry there were high, and I did not even apply when I was in Standard 7 initially. A teacher reviewed my application and felt that I (and one or two others) should apply.

On arrival at this school, it was palpably different from the very start. There were six classes of 40 in each year. I was in Form 1A, and my form teacher was a British white person. The school had amazing sports facilities, including a swimming pool. The pupils came from a range of families and means, but were all Asian or African. Many travelled from up country, some on a daily basis. I will never forget the boy who ran six miles each way every day, just to comply with both his family commitments and the school time-table. He had no problem on sports day. Indeed in the 1972 Olympic Games, several members of the Kenyan team were school boys from my school!

At the end of the first term, there were exams. I wanted to do my best, and the thought of losing the lead position was a reality check. However, I did manage to get top scores that term. At the end of the year, no one was more surprised than me when I was top of the year – out of 240 pupils. I was able to carry this on, in fact, for the whole two years I was there.

During my second year there, our family was reclassified as visitors in my country of birth. My passport had a visitor's visa stamped on it, just like any tourist on holiday in Kenya. My father needed a work permit to be in gainful employment as a tourist, though he had lived there for 52 years by then. Later that year, we were informed by the authorities that my father's work permit would not be renewed; we were welcome to stay on as tourists. At that point, the British High Commission was not prepared to even accept an application for a visa to move to the United Kingdom. It was only when the work permit actually expired that the application would be accepted, followed by a processing time of nine months. We lived off saving for those nine months, so that when we finally did heart-wrenchingly leave behind a home, life, family and friends and a social life and fly to the United Kingdom in September 1973, we landed at Heathrow airport with £40 in my father's pocket. I was in proud possession of a school leaving certificate from my high school.

By late October 1973, we were renting a house in an East London borough. I personally went to the education offices to apply for schooling. I was sent to a high school, a 2,500 pupil comprehensive. I spent a day there, and was shocked at the general standards of attention, discipline and aspiration. The next day I went straight back to the education office to complain that the school was not good enough in my view. Predictably, they paid no attention to the views of a newly arrived fifteen year old. A chance discussion with our landlord resulted in advice to approach a local grammar school for boys. Again I personally arranged an appointment to meet the headmaster there, and was dismissed on the basis that he could only follow orders from the education authority. I had to go to the comprehensive.

It was a recently converted comprehensive, having previously been a grammar school. At my assessment, the assistant head asked me a little about the physics I had learned, as that was his subject. He was a reasonable man, who soon became the acting head within days of my starting school there. However, an enduring memory for me is the casual way in which he put aside my leaving certificate from Nairobi, without even looking at it. It was at that time one of my most important achievements.

Following a brief discussion, it was agreed that I should not bother with history or geography as I had hitherto studied Africa, and did struggle with European studies. I was to study English, mathematics, physics, chemistry and biology. Even the standard of French was not as good as in Kenya.

The killer blow was when I discovered that I was put into the bottom stream for every subject. I had not been formally tested – it was assumed that that was all I was good enough for.

The following week, I approached the physics teacher and informed him that I would pursue my O-level on my own. I had the excuse of being brought up on traditional physics rather than the Nuffield method they were doing. I got myself a copy of the standard text book and studied it in my own time. For biology I was put into the fourth and fifth years, because of overlap. However, we soon realised that the fourth year was doing what we in Nairobi had done in our first year. So I then concentrated on the fifth year alone.

One day I had not done the fourth year biology work, because the teacher had established that I did not need to pursue that year any more. However, I was summoned by the head of Biology and informed that I should consider CSEs rather than O-levels.

In the event I got A grades in all the O-level exams in the summer of 1974, six months before I would have if still in Kenya. However, the arts and languages were sacrificed.

I went on to the sixth form, studying physics, chemistry and biology. An interesting social shift now happened.

On arrival at the school in 1973, I was one of fewer than ten Asian pupils in the school. Being harassed was a fact of life, though not everybody was guilty. I am sure there are many examples of the reverse as well. What was fascinating to me was the particular form of it. The school was over 90 per cent Jewish. The Asians were therefore subjected to racial abuse, and a more subtle form of exclusion from not being Jewish.

At the end of the lower sixth year we did exams. I scored highest in all three subjects. Suddenly they all wanted to be even more friendly. I was pleased to gain acceptance by whatever means it took, at that stage. I was a foreign adolescent, recently arrived. Apart from the migration, clearly other changes and anxieties were in play in me just like in anyone else at that age.

When it came to filling in the UCCA forms, there was little guidance from most teachers. The sixth form master, who was also my biology teacher, was different. He recognised something in me. He gave me mock interviews, and taking into account both my in-decision and aptitude for things scientific, advised me to apply for medical school on the grounds that if I got in and wanted to change, it would not be a problem to give up a place in medical school. The other way round would be uphill. So I did. I was offered a conditional place at a hospital Medical School in London. I went on to acquire the neces-sary grades and a new life began at University. I had been in the country for three years then, and felt fairly well assimilated, but preserved my cultural identity by being involved in Indian music and so on. My apparently double life in this way continues to date. I am married to a lovely English woman, and have three fantastic daughters. I do not push the Indian-ness on anyone, but am quite protective, even defensive about it if provoked.

I was lucky enough to follow my chosen speciality and become a consultant in ortho-paedic surgery, which I find immensely rewarding. However, on the whole I feel that whilst the solid foundations from Nairobi were invaluable in that period of turmoil, any success I harnessed cannot be credited to my high school in London – it was in spite of it.

Gus

I came to the UK from Argentina in 1976 when I was thirteen. I missed the first two years of English schooling because of problems with age equivalence. I did three months of secondary schooling there. I went into Year 9 with O-levels coming up reasonably soon but I had missed the whole of Year 7 and Year 8, and being new to English at the time I had to learn everything for that.

I went straight into a London school. There were no other Spanish speakers, though lots of other foreign students. I say lots but compared to today it was probably quite minimal.

My two best friends were from Cyprus and Trinidad, I think that we were quite an isolated group at that time – foreign students were quite a new thing.

We were withdrawn from languages, so I didn't do French for example, but did what was called special English. I can't really remember at which point I began to understand things, and how much it was down to the special English help and how much you just absorb the language. Or was it by osmosis?! I remember going to those lessons and enjoying them and I'm guessing they must have helped, but I can't say. We had a text book and we used to try and develop dialogues based for example on how our weekend was.

I initially came to England for only one year. The reason we came was that my mum was a scientist and got offered a one year post in England. But in Argentina there was a military coup, so we couldn't go back and it meant we were going to be staying. As a thirteen year old I was dead opposed to the idea of going to school in England. I couldn't see the point of just going to school for a year. I know I kicked up a huge fuss about going to school. I hated the idea. I think I was a very unhappy child at the time. It was quite unsettling being pulled out of Argentina and coming to England.

My first impressions of England were that it was very drab; the country looked very grey and all the houses were the same, rows and rows of houses – that's completely different from Argentina, and I just found it really depressing. I've got one brother who adapted more quickly than I did. He was younger, he was eleven years old and went straight into Year 7 so he picked up secondary from the start. I think he found it a bit easier than I did.

I had only done a little bit of secondary school in Argentina – the secondary schools there are very, very different from here. It's like going into WH Smiths, then going into a car dealership so there isn't a direct comparison. As an example, there, you sit in your own class, on your chair the whole day and teachers come and go. Different subject teachers come and teach you so it's the teachers that move round. There weren't resourced areas for particular subjects such as science or technology – so it was all very much chalk and talk. Everything is about memorising facts. Everything is different, the whole thing is completely different. Obviously, once I got into the English system I much preferred it but at the time it was a big shock. A culture shock. I was only going to be here for a year, I didn't see why I should be going through this. However, I was always a good student and always did what was asked of me.

Setting was completely new to us, so the idea of being set by ability didn't happen in Argentina, you were taught in your form group. In maths, I was put into a class for a week then moved into another class, then another class. I didn't know why I was being moved and why my maths teacher kept changing. They may have explained but I didn't understand. Later I found that I had been climbing up sets all the way through, because the school found that I was quite mathematically able and it was my English holding me back. I ended up in set 2, that was the highest I ever got but it was the weirdest thing being taken to different maths classes each week!

I was entered for my exams in Year 11. At the time we did CSEs and O-levels. My teachers decided that my English wasn't strong enough to sit O-levels, so I was entered for CSEs in all subjects except maths, which I passed, and strangely enough, English (which I failed). This shows how clued up the school was! I took CSEs because my teachers explained to me that if you get a CSE grade 1 it's equivalent to an O-level, so that didn't disappoint me. I did an O-level in Spanish in Year 10 – the first student in that school to ever do an O-level in Year 10. They trialled this with me and it worked as I obviously got an A! Taking CSEs didn't affect my further education because we had a sixth form at our school and I was told that if I got four or five CSEs grade 1, I'd be able to do A-levels in whatever I wanted, which was fine. They regarded me as an individual. They knew that if I was capable of getting the five I'd be able to do A-levels, and that's what happened.

The social aspects of school I found difficult. I don't think this had anything to do with being a foreign student though. I had hair which used to stick up in knots, terrible acne all over my face and I had national health glasses, with sellotape on the end – so I was the biggest target in the whole school! On top of that I didn't speak the language. Kids would come to me and urge me to 'say this' – obviously they were swearing. So I wasn't happy. I was missing my Argentinean friends. We are different in Argentina, we are very tactile, it's just the way we are. There are differences with the culture.

I think it's the inclusion, the encouragement, the actually asking about you as a person, an individual, how you're getting on, that made the difference. That's what motivates you to want to work for a person. All kids will work for teachers they like, it's something you can hold on to. You can only really hold onto things like kindness, when you don't understand the words or the language. That makes a big difference.

Looking back, I don't know that the language held me back in any way. I think I would have achieved the same wherever I was. I'm not really an ambitious person. The fact that I took my CSEs and got grade 1 in all of them (so that they were equivalent to O-levels) within a few years of arriving, is a major achievement. Coming to England gave me the opportunities to do with my life what I wanted because in Argentina, you could be the hardest working, most intelligent person, but the opportunities just weren't there. The system works differently. It's much more difficult to make it there.

Unlike the adults now reflecting on their experience, children generally have to accept the experience of isolation. The following three incidents reflect the need for awareness.

A young person, one of a few bilingual learners in a suburban school, when interviewed for research on schools with isolated learners did not expect anyone to draw on her life stories. She started to speak about Ramadan and very patiently explained what it was. If she had talked about Ramadan in school classes she might have assumed the interviewer knew about it.

Children were asked to talk about life in a Southern Indian village on the strength of a holiday with relatives in the Punjab in Northern India.

A Year 2 bilingual learner moved from one part of the authority to another. Staff at the new school didn't have access to his records and so didn't realise that his language was a southern Indian one, completely different to a more familiar northern Indian one.

These observations, relating to one sub-continent of origin only, provide evidence of some of the issues affecting isolated bilingual learners. Hampshire, the focus for this book, illustrates a variety of positive outcomes.

Successful schools scoop up isolated bilingual learners and include them in their holistic philosophy and practice of *Every Child Matters: change for children* (DfES, 2004b) and therefore 'every bilingual child matters'. In a successful school it doesn't matter whether the children and young people are newly arrived with previous education or with none. It doesn't matter whether the children have been in settings or schools for over five years and are therefore considered to be advanced bilingual learners or for a shorter time. It doesn't matter whether the children have been at the same school or a variety of schools in the UK or overseas. Perhaps above all it doesn't matter if there is one or more than one child speaking the same language and from the same background in the school.

Successful schools implement appropriate provision and help isolated bilingual learners achieve across all year groups. They adapt provision to meet the needs of their isolated bilingual learners. They do not expect isolated bilingual learners to have to fit into a setting or school which remains unchanged by the experience. Indeed, they will learn all they can about how to enhance provision for all children and young people by tailoring provision to meet individual needs.

Successful settings, schools and colleges can be isolated themselves. They may or may not have back-up from a central specialist Ethnic Minority Achievement (EMA) service. Staff working with isolated bilingual learners, particularly if bilingual themselves, may be isolated too. Families may or may not have community contacts, for example at community language classes, within reach.

At the beginning of the 1990s just over 100 bilingual learners, all isolated, were identified in Hampshire local authority data. As this book is being written, over 1,000 new arrival referrals to the central EMA service have been admitted into schools in a year.

Isolated bilingual learners form part of a continuum of bilingual learners. There is a wealth of literature which discusses theory, planning and practice applicable to all. But there are specific issues affecting isolated bilingual learners which are new to setting, school and college staff, hereafter referred to as school staff, working with bilingual learners for the first time. Staff want guidance and assistance. Key actions in successful schools across the board are maximising use of staff, ensuring high expectations, tackling racism, including provision for isolated bilingual learners in self-evaluation and tracking, joining up with other schools to address issues and analysing data for implementing further improvement.

There comes a time when schools realise they have isolated bilingual learners. The numbers of bilingual learners in the school may grow but the isolation for each one may remain the same. Schools work on principles, strategies and development of consistent practice. *Every Child Matters* (DfES, 2004b) begins to mean 'every isolated bilingual learner matters'. This book is for staff in those schools.

1

Isolated bilingual learners

Liz Statham

Then and now

Fifteen years ago the concept of isolated bilingual learners as a particular group was emerging. Factors affecting these learners were identified, conferences addressed the issues and Local Education Authority (LEA) Bilingual Learners services were established in suburban and rural areas where previously there had only been emergency responses from the nearest urban services.

Researchers from the University of Luton investigated the situation of ethnic minority pupils in mainly white schools. For the research, a mainly white school was defined as a school in which only 4-6 per cent of pupils were from ethnic minority backgrounds. They found that by 1996-1997 there were only eight small LEAs with very few or no schools with a significant proportion of ethnic minority pupils (more than 4%) across the country. The researchers suggested that:

> the great majority of teachers across the country may now expect to work with minority ethnic pupils at some point in their career, and mainly white schools in almost all areas may expect to admit minority ethnic pupils more frequently than in the past. (Cline *et al*, 2002)

Even since 2002 the lines between provision for isolated bilingual learners and new arrivals have blurred. There is a very well received *New Arrivals Excellence Programme* (DfES and DCSF, 2007) to draw on. This includes examples of inclusive schools responding to the needs of isolated bilingual learners. Nevertheless, isolated bilingual learners are not necessarily new arrivals and new arrivals are not necessarily isolated.

At a time when the spread of isolated bilingual learners has increased, it is timely to re-visit the issues identified from the early 1990s onwards and offer examples of good principles and practice in a large county in England.

In 2006, the school-aged ethnic minority population in England was 21 per cent and 18 per cent for primary and secondary children and young people respectively. Concentrations of ethnic minority children and young people in urban areas contribute to these figures but there are isolated bilingual learners in towns and suburbs as well as rural areas. In 2005, there was only one school in Hampshire with over 20 per cent of ethnic minority children on roll. In 2006, there were ten schools with over 20 per cent.

Informal contacts from all over the country testify to the fact that families from, for example, Eastern Europe or a wide range of African countries, are not settling solely in urban areas. Families may be joining established communities and attending settings, schools or colleges with experience of meeting the needs of all learners. Families may be joining one or two other families with the same language and cultural background in an area. A family or an unaccompanied child seeking asylum may be paving the way in an area by educating a receptive setting, school or college about their background and needs.

Isolated bilingual learners
So what does it mean to be an isolated bilingual learner? In percentage terms most people would think of under 10 per cent ethnic minority children or young people in a setting, school or college as isolated. No institution intentionally seeks to isolate a particular group. Children and young people may feel, however, that their educational and cultural background is not reflected in their place of learning. They may face an increased risk of racism on their way to and from school or in school. They may find that there is no community language class near enough for them to attend easily. Above all, they may not have their first language recognised and valued.

Investing in achievement

At first glance you would think that bilingual learners in a situation where there is a high percentage of ethnic minority children and young people would fare best. There are likely to be other children who speak their language. School staff are used to admitting, inducting and supporting children from a wide range of backgrounds. There is an investment for class teachers in providing supportive strategies for English as an additional language when the majority of the class is bilingual. A wide range of levels amongst the bilingual members of the class will provide models of English for other bilingual learners.

But there are advantages to being an isolated bilingual learner. First and foremost you probably have at least 29 other English speakers to provide models for you. As Wong Filmore says:

> Very few children can resist these forces and avoid the linguistic assimilation that is an inevitable part of growing up in the society. (Wong Filmore, 1980)

Provided that English is being learned for learning that situation is fine. If it is English on its own and de-contextualised from curriculum subjects that is being learned then isolated bilingual learners 'frequently derive no benefit from school other than learning English'. (Wong Filmore, 1980)

All bilingual learners are faced with a moving target in the sense that their monolingual peers do not stand still (Thomas and Collier, 1997). All bilingual learners do not have the luxury of time to learn English before starting to learn everything else that is required. It is vital for class and subject teachers to create opportunities for both learning and language development. It is the case that when one English learner is amongst 30 then the teacher's role has less to do with specific language instruction and more to do with ensuring that there are possibilities for interaction.

Since an individual class or subject teacher may have less intrinsic investment in one or two bilingual learners in their class than all 28 or 29 monolingual learners, it is important that groupings are created with high expectations of isolated bilingual learners learning from their peers, that collaborative activities are in place and that isolated children and young people are not subject to racism.

Whole school approaches

Interaction can't be developed by one member of staff sitting beside an isolated bilingual learner, perhaps in the hope that kindness and easy English will pave the way to learning. There has to be a holistic embedding of *Every Child Matters* (DfES, 2004b) so that parents, administrative staff, lunchtime supervisors, personal and careers advisers and local authority personnel all play a part in ensuring that education and social care is of the same quality for isolated bilingual learners as it is for any child.

That is why the focus of this book is about building capacity across settings, schools and colleges. There are chapters on working across the authority to spread good practice, on maximising impact of teaching assistants, on involving parents, on implementing appropriate assessment, on reinforcing the distinction between bilingual learners and bilingual learners with special educational needs and considering learning disability issues. Last, but not least, there is a chapter on involving young people in tackling racism.

There are no chapters on planning language development across the curriculum. That issue has been covered superbly in Maggie Gravelle's book *Planning for Bilingual Learners* (Gravelle, 2000) and in the Primary National Strategy toolkit *Excellence and Enjoyment: learning and teaching for bilingual children in the primary years – professional development materials* (DfES, 2006). These resources provide a comprehensive guide to teaching and learning, particularly for advanced bilingual learners and not just for the primary phase. The *New Arrivals Excellence Programme* (DfES and DCSF, 2007) provides guidance for schools working with new arrivals to the country whether in small or large numbers. The focus on teaching and learning is a vital one but in an isolated situation takes second place to a focus on access and integration.

With increased numbers of new arrivals into the UK, in isolated areas as well as areas with large numbers of bilingual learners, the temptation is to shift back to a focus, common in the 1960s, on learning English in the early stages. Then, a concentration on initial stages was very important. It reflected the belief that pupils would be absorbed into mainstream life and learning of the school once they had acquired English. It was commonly held that English needed to be taught in steps and stages following a grammatical progression from easiest to most complex. It meant that those steps and stages of English did not fit neatly with learning and teaching going on in classrooms and therefore children were taught separately by language specialists. Language-structured teaching went hand in hand with withdrawal provision.

Bourne found that one of the key policy changes of the 1980s was:

> to take account of language diversity in the pupil population as the classroom norm rather than the exception: in order to give access to the curriculum for all pupils by providing for diverse language needs. (Bourne, 1989)

It began to seem nonsensical to take pupils away from the sources of meaning ie classrooms where learning is concretely and visually supported and where peers adapt their language as appropriate to meet the needs of classmates.

It is even more nonsensical for isolated bilingual learners to be removed from such positive learning environments. To this day it is hard to challenge the apparently commonsense view that learning English must come before letting children and young people learn the English they need for the curriculum by actually learning the language needed for curriculum tasks.

However, the commonsense view must be challenged. Leung (2007) has pointed out that in the 21st century bilingual learners are expected to learn English while engaged in curriculum subject work and teachers are expected to see English as an Additional Language (EAL) development as part of the overall learning needs of individual students. Conceptually, additional language teaching and learning are considered as an inherent part of the wider communication and participatory processes in the classroom.

Leung argues that this person-orientated perspective on EAL has, so far, tended to focus on making the classroom processes 'accessible', that is, helping students with EAL with content-learning activities through a combination of hands-on activities, visuals and so on. The central assumption is that EAL development will follow active participation in the curriculum but Leung argues that a person-orientated EAL perspective focused on classroom communication and participatory process is conceptually ill-equipped to address additional language teaching and learning issues adequately. This is particularly the case as the EAL expertise base in schools has reduced and therefore the language development focus within the curriculum may be at risk. Pressures arise when instant success in English is expected.

In isolated situations, a language development focus within the curriculum has had to develop without specialists in each school. What has had to happen and what needs to happen is a focus on embedding the successful teaching and learning strategies for language development in the curriculum as well as the person-oriented access for isolated bilingual learners across the board; not enough specialist teachers can be provided in all isolated situations.

Specialist staff in isolated situations have therefore attempted to embed access and integration and are trying to avoid pressure to return to induction units where de-contextualised English is taught. Rather they are trying to build learning and language development capacity in schools. This capacity has not as yet been fully realised in all situations.

Nevertheless, just as staff working with isolated bilingual learners drew on the experience of staff working in the inner cities during the 1980s, perhaps now all staff working with bilingual learners can draw on the approaches necessary in isolated areas where specialist teachers, teaching assistants, bilingual assistants, researchers and senior leaders in schools have to work together to provide access and teaching and learning across the curriculum.

Hampshire

Provision for isolated bilingual learners across the 540 schools of the local authority is not further behind inner city areas in principle but it has to be said that it is still inconsistent across the board.

One of the worries expressed in 1992, at the start of the specialist service in its own right in the authority, still remains although much eased:

■ isolation from religious, cultural and community activities or considerable travel to get to them

The majority of concerns have been largely resolved with changing tides or concentrated efforts:

- lack of peer or adult support in first language(s) in schools

- likelihood of stress reactions for some newly arrived isolated bilingual learners

- embarrassment and reluctance to acknowledge cultural and linguistic aspects of identity, affecting pupils' views of themselves as learners

- potential concentration on spoken language in school initially, with subsequent potential gaps in written language at a later stage

- concerns about appropriate assessment particularly at early stages of operating in two languages

- concerns about transition ie that records in many cases do not show pupils as bilingual learners

- little chance to diagnose a pupil who appears to be struggling as having anything other than learning difficulties

The focus of the book is on implementing good practice for isolated bilingual learners, child after child, school after school and year after year. The chapters reflect the principles of holistic inclusive provision and painstaking capacity building.

The vignettes interspersed throughout this book are extracts from teachers' and classroom assistants' journals as they grapple with the issues of whole school change to provide access for isolated bilingual learners and consistency of approach in teaching and learning. The journals form part of their coursework for Teaching English as an Additional Language (TEAL), a course part-funded by the Teachers Development Agency and accredited at master's level by the University of Portsmouth. The participants are developing infrastructures for building capacity in schools. They are leading teachers, unqualified teachers and teaching assistants. Their practice is underpinned by an unshakeable belief in the value of bilingualism, high expectations and a realisation that everyone in school has a part to play.

The practice is not yet perfect but the messages are getting through. The vignettes start with a secondary mainstream teacher reflecting on access for bilingual learners in her school.

I can see that my early concerns are to do with feeling overwhelmed by the number of issues I have to deal with as a mainstream classroom teacher. I think one of the reasons I became more relaxed about EAL learners in my class is partly because of some reading I did about being bilingual. I also came across an article which echoed some of my thoughts and feelings:

> ...teaching EAL learners continues to be a daunting responsibility for teachers who in the past decade, have been subject to significant and demanding innovations in the education system. Asked how they felt about this responsibility, one teacher commented, 'apprehension and fear that one won't be able to...that it will be an overwhelming task...' (Franson, 1999)

Reading this, I felt less guilty about resenting all the demands placed on my shoulders. On reading *Being Bilingual* by Alladina (1995) I began to perceive being a bilingual learner in a different way, seeing it less as a problem to be over-come and more as a normal way of being and living for the majority of people. Most people on earth are bilingual; actually it is me as a monolingual person who is in the minority when you take a global perspective. This is not to underestimate the challenge for both pupils and teachers in mainstream classrooms, but I think this wider view is helpful; somehow it removes unnecessary pressure.

I recall a conversation I had with a colleague during a shared break-time duty. She said, 'How can someone bring their child to another country and plonk them into an English speaking classroom – I could not do it to my child'. I think this comment might be interpreted as lacking in awareness of the reality of the lives of millions of families. It is economics that is at play here, not lack of concern by the parents for the children in the families of economic migrants, refugees and asylum seekers.

I discussed this with my partner. We came to the conclusion that, as Alladina says, some parents send their children, at great expense, to another country to learn a second language. Also, because of the cognitive advantages in learning to speak another language, some parents send their children to private bilingual nurseries and schools.

I thought about my own school and realised there were no visible positive state-ments around the school that said to a pupil coming from another country that they and their language were welcome. I recall a lesson which was noted in my journal. It was a PSHE (personal, social and health education) lesson. Having learnt that using one's own language is extremely desirable when learning in another lan-guage, I decided that two newly arrived Polish boys could write about the topic (I think it was a letter from a young person to a problem page about a drug problem) in Polish. From the back of the classroom one of the other members of the group, a British-born white boy, said 'They can't write in Polish they're in England now'. This illustrates the views of many of the local white pupils towards ethnic minority children within the school, it is not always particularly positive. I also think that because I was very sure about my rationale for allowing the Polish boys to speak and write in Polish I was able to assertively and confidently deal with the dissenting voice.

This quote from a novel called *Unless* by Carol Shields (2002), a Canadian writer, I think sums up how enriching an experience it can be to be bilingual. It describes beautifully how learning in two languages can clarify and reinforce meanings:

> Oddly the epic confusion of my early years was not caused but rather mitigated by immersion in two languages; doubleness clarified the world; *la chaise*, chair; *le rideau*, curtain; *être*, to be; *le chien*, a dog. Every object has an echo, an explanation. Meaning had two feet, two etymological stems. I swam in English, a relaxed backstroke, but stood up to my hips in French.

Liz Statham is inspector/adviser for the Hampshire Ethnic Minority Achievement Service (EMA) Service. She has worked as an EAL teacher and trainer in Melbourne, Haringey and Hampshire. Her 1993 PhD thesis from the University of Southampton is entitled Scattered in the Mainstream: educational provision for isolated bilingual learners.

2

Building capacity across the authority

Liz Statham

Inclusion

Schools increasingly manage their own affairs so where does that leave isolated bilingual learners? If schools take a holistic, inclusive approach it leaves them very well placed. In these cases every individual child or young person matters.

Leaders in such schools set the tone. They often have to model for administrative staff a welcome for a family into school and community. They often have to model for parents a welcome for a family into the playground. They make links with all possible sources of help within the community. They find staff to support individuals in mainstream classes. They welcome parents in as volunteers and, if possible, workers in the school. They encourage and value the use of first languages. They build capacity by spreading the messages about learning in whatever language being a priority across the whole school staff through practical training, shadowing and induction. They follow the principle that encouraging interaction is more important in an isolated situation than specific English instruction.

These principles dovetail with thinking highlighted in the National Strategies and the Department for Education and Skills' programme to raise ethnic minority achievement *Aiming High* (2005a). The starting points of linking listening, speaking, reading and writing , providing visual support, collaborative work and staging tasks are considered routine good practice for all children. An additional specialist aspect is to analyse what language is needed to access and undertake curriculum tasks. This aspect has been highlighted in the Primary National Strategy's toolkit *Excellence and Enjoyment: learning and teaching for bilingual children in the primary years – professional development materials* (DfES, 2006) so that the method can be adopted by mainstream staff.

There should now be no tension between meeting the needs of isolated bilingual learners and all children in schools. Provided that language demands of tasks are analysed in curriculum planning then isolated bilingual learners will benefit from National Strategies approaches, as will all bilingual learners and indeed all learners.

Consistency

Provision to provide access to the curriculum is not fully in place across many authorities with isolated bilingual learners. There are pockets of good practice. Inevitably perhaps, schools facing Office for Standards in Education (Ofsted) inspections have priorities other than provision for isolated bilingual learners on their minds. It is often said that how a society treats its refugees is an indication of its level of civilisation. The same could be said of a society's treatment of its isolated bilingual learners.

In only nine out of 50 Hampshire inspection reports checked in 2005-2006 was there any mention of standards achieved by bilingual learners. This means that achievement may not have been a significant issue in a large number of schools' Self Evaluation Forms (SEFs).

The initiatives taken to embed the DFES and Ofsted's *New Relationships with Schools* (2004) which seeks to challenge and support schools through a single conversation with a School Improvement Partner (SIP), improved inspection, school self evaluation and communication can play a significant part as messages about raising achievement of isolated bilingual learners can be endorsed by SIPs, leading teachers and targeted advisory support for specific schools.

Developments across Hampshire are still patchy. In two areas there are leading teachers for primary and a lead professional for secondary schools. They develop a whole school focus on meeting the needs of isolated bilingual learners in their schools and then in a cluster of schools. They deliver very well received training on ethnic minority achievement co-ordination in schools, on using *A Language in Common* (QCA, 2000) for assessment, on analysing the language demands of tasks, on staging access to curriculum tasks and on running integrated homework clubs and developing parental links. They work closely with, or are themselves, senior managers in schools.

One of the key initiatives for lead teachers and professionals as well as specialist teachers in the Ethnic Minority Achievement (EMA) service is contributing to schools' SEFs. To help with this process the service has developed guidance with a matrix drawing on the work of several authorities and following the OfSTED self-evaluation criteria (www.hants.gov.uk/education/ema). Use of the matrix ensures that even one bilingual learner is considered in a school's analysis and factors leading to under-achievement, achievement in line with peers or achievement of full potential and more are considered.

Information about achievement is shared with School Improvement Partners (SIPs) in as many schools as possible so that they can question schools about their analysis and move schools to identifying their own priorities in identifying and meeting needs of isolated bilingual learners. That process sounds straightforward but in an authority with 540 schools there are also up to 540 SIPs. Opportunities have to be found for aligning EMA specialists with SIPs and also with subject specialists. In this respect the National Strategies EMA hub developments are timely and helpful. The hubs allow primary and secondary strategy consultants to meet EMA specialists to share planning for developing alignment in the local authority.

Interagency working

Increasingly alignment amongst a range of agencies is needed to implement *Every Child Matters* (DfES, 2004b) There are three areas and eleven districts in Hampshire. There are four key areas of interagency work; common assessment framework (CAF), children's centres, extended services and the work of locality teams.

Issues affecting isolated bilingual learners need to be heard and acted on across the board. A key appointment has been that of a Black and

Minority Ethnic (BME) Children's Development Officer. Her priorities have been those of the authority's *Change For Children* programme (Hampshire County Council, 2005) and the *Children and Young People's Plan* (Hampshire County Council, 2006). She has kept the EMA service informed about training, for example for Common Assessment Framework (CAF) completer courses and has kept other agencies informed about EMA provision. Perhaps inevitably the amount of information is enormous and it takes time to adjust priorities and to decide who will pick up on particular aspects of interagency work.

Self-help is still needed. An example of an innovative capacity building collaboration between the Ethnic Minority Achievement Service, three primary phase leading teachers in EAL and a secondary phase lead professional focuses on training young interpreters (www.hants.gov.uk/education/ema).

This young interpreter initiative is not the only example of sustained project work. There are examples of practice from other authorities which contribute to breaking down barriers for isolated bilingual learners. Devon local authority service for instance provides video conferencing for isolated bilingual learners to talk to other speakers of the same language. The service also provides one-off days for all the children speaking the same language within a reasonable travel to session area to attend an art workshop with one monolingual friend each. At first glance this day might seem a distraction from curriculum work in schools. The impact on integration however is considerable as all the work is collaborative.

On one of these days the Polish speaking participants were asked to work with monolingual friends to select photos of Poland at the time of the second world war for an information book that could then be used as a resource in schools across the authority. Art therapy sessions might seem a distraction from the curriculum but when children, sometimes Unaccompanied Children Seeking Asylum (UCSA) troubled by events in their country of origin or journey to Devon, have to negotiate where their part of a picture fits into a whole collage then the impact on interaction is significant.

14-19

What happens to isolated 14-19 year olds at a time when the curriculum is changing with diplomas being made available to cross the academic and vocational divide? Unless lucky, such bilingual learners have until recently been caught at the border between school and college provision. Schools do not receive funding for students beyond the age of 16 and so colleges have been hesitant about receiving students without a standard of English perceived good enough for access to existing courses.

This transition barrier has been in sharp contrast to colleges in inner city areas where language and learning have proceeded hand in hand whether for academic or vocational studies. Indeed in some colleges within an isolated bilingual catchment area there are entry tests in English for entry to courses. Colleges are rightly concerned about helping students meet English requirements for university. Historically, entry has been gained through the English for Speakers of other Languages (ESOL) route as colleges in isolated areas have received most of their other students with GCSEs or repeating the GCSE course normally taken at age 16.

The ESOL route is linked to the adult National Curriculum. This ESOL strand is primarily designed, as Leung (2007) notes for:

> migrant workers, refugees and asylum seekers, and members of settled minority communities who 'work long and irregular hours and therefore cannot attend classes regularly'. (DfES, 2001)

So as such:

> unlike the school situation where English learning is meant to be embedded in subject or curriculum learning, the ESOL provision in further and adult education is very much a distinct and time-tabled subject. (Leung, 2007)

Leung asks if such a curriculum is suitable for the needs of a young person who has already studied in a local school for, say, five years and will now follow a university matriculation course?

> And would such disjuncture in provision for 16-18 year olds not undermine the respective stated educational bases and claims of legitimacy for both school EAL and ESOL policies? (Leung, 2007)

When numbers are low it is currently easier to ask students to fit into existing college requirements than to ask for the provision to adapt to the needs of students and solve the disjuncture Leung describes. This means that in some cases students are required to spend a year studying ESOL as a subject before they have access to pre-university courses.

In Hampshire there have been some initiatives to bridge the gaps. There are examples of more flexible provision where numbers of isolated students rise. The vignette below describes how one lead EAL professional has reflected on the curriculum options open to newly arrived isolated bilingual learners aged 14-16 in her school.

Of the many possible curriculum models for newly arrived bilingual students in KS4 this extract focuses on three. All assume that students will for the majority of the time attend mainstream lessons in the full range of subjects.

The first option, a mainstream timetable with in-class support, where students sink or swim, has until now been the only option in School V. The school endeavours to provide appropriate support through deployment of learning support colleagues, peripatetic bilingual assistants, and extra voluntary tutorials. Teachers have to consider in advance the language requirements of the lesson for bilingual students and aim to model effective use of vocabulary and structures.

Two clear advantages of this model are that bilingual students are from the start in lessons across the curriculum and can therefore begin to fill any gaps in their learning left when transferring between countries, education systems and schools; and that students who speak only English generally benefit greatly from the increased language awareness in lessons, as topic words are made explicit and key phrases modelled.

Other strategies include using a wide variety of visuals, for example symbols, diagrams, models and photographs, as well as the use of videos, drama and ICT. Teachers may prepare simplified or highlighted texts and some may provide a list of keywords in advance of the lesson. Peers with the same language as a new arrival may be able to explain main points and concepts, though this must never be allowed to become a burden on the established student.

Difficulties with this model at school V include the limited bilingual assistant time available and the fact that many teachers feel ill-equipped to meet the needs of older students in the earlier stages of learning English. Further training and resource development is needed to enable all colleagues to feel confident in their ability adequately to support bilingual learners.

The second alternative is to offer an induction timetable during which students attend some mainstream classes and also a part-time course aimed at supporting a smoother transition into education in the UK and to learning through English.

This would include introducing key language, concepts and skills from all subject areas and an introduction to the necessary study skills for success at GCSE. Students would transfer after a period of time to a full mainstream timetable. A similar induction programme for Key Stage 3 has been run elsewhere with great success (*New Arrivals Excellence Programme* DfES and DCSF, 2007)

Before offering an induction course, the first requirement at School V would be joint preparation time for curriculum colleagues and EAL teachers for lesson planning and resource design. Schools should remember that students who have previously been in continuous education are likely already to have acquired a considerable amount of subject knowledge and in some areas may be ahead of their British peers (Stanton, 1999). This must be taken into account to ensure that individual students can build upon their prior learning.

The third approach is for bilingual students to spend an option per week throughout KS4 in a language study and study support class, receiving additional guidance with coursework, exam skills and perhaps own language teaching. Schools should reflect carefully before placing students on such a programme as it inevitably entails withdrawal from another curriculum subject. This remains a supportive option for those needing additional assistance to access the full range of curriculum materials and may be an appropriate choice for students arriving late in Year 10 or Year 11, who over and above any language needs will have missed some GCSE course teaching.

A consideration for schools would be which mainstream subject to replace. This will be different for each student and timetabling would therefore need to be flexible. One assumption is that for students learning English, embarking upon another language at the same time would be inappropriate. Research has refuted this, showing that in fact the linguistic awareness of bilingual students makes them efficient learners of additional languages. (DfES, 2004a). With few exceptions, School V policy is that all bilingual students should study a language and recent exam results have shown this to be the right decision for most students. Equally, humanities subjects, while demanding high levels of literacy, are frequently highly relevant to new entrants, allowing them to draw upon first hand experience of the country, situation or religious practice studied. Schools must therefore guide students according to their strengths and be prepared to structure their timetables accordingly.

To support language development, students sharing a common first language could work together, using their first language as appropriate to investigate further concepts or themes covered in mainstream classes. Schools should endeavour to identify appropriate persons who could, after training, offer first language literacy support to students and the opportunity to use first language in an education context as acknowledged in the DfES's *Excellence and enjoyment – the toolkit for bilingual children in the primary years* (DfES, 2006)

Different curriculum models may be considered more suitable for students arriving at different stages of KS4, especially during Year 11 when rapid progress in English and curriculum learning is crucial. Individual students' aspirations and future plans must be foremost when making KS4 decisions. While it is generally best to place students in age-appropriate classes (DfES, 2005a) many students from other countries may not expect this and families sometimes request that a student arriving halfway through the Key Stage should start in the year below, allowing two full years for GCSE preparation. A more long-term approach, however, would be for students to start their GCSE courses at school and continue at college.

The question of qualifications is another consideration for schools following the language study and study support option. Should this option lead to accreditation, or should it exist as a study support and language enrichment option with the sole aim of enhancing students' performance in other curriculum subjects? Raising achievement through effective support may well be seen to be sufficient justification for the course. The current emphasis on Contextual Value Added student performance, demonstrating a school's impact on individual student attainment, and particularly the breakdown of these figures according to ethnicity, may increase interest from some schools in own language GCSEs. However, entering a student for any examination must depend upon his or her own ability and needs.

First language GCSEs are available in many, though by no means all, languages and the opportunities for advanced level qualifications are limited. English language qualifications for bilingual students exist but with numerous restrictions; the International GCSE English for EAL is available only overseas or to students in private sector schools; some awarding bodies require teachers to undertake additional training to gain centre accreditation; and other examinations sometimes taken by bilingual students are intended for British adults who have not previously achieved literacy qualifications, and are therefore of limited relevance to bilingual young people. Some courses focus on English for living in the UK rather than for educational purposes, while other more academic courses are aimed at students in sixth form colleges and universities.

When choosing qualifications, schools should consider whether the examination content is accessible; students may be disadvantaged by culturally Euro or UK-centric papers if they have only recently moved to the UK. Schools should ascertain which qualifications are recognised by local colleges and universities and may even wish to make enquiries at centres of learning in the student's home country if his or her residency in the UK is likely to be short-term.

The choice of pathway and appropriate qualifications will be different for each student. A one size fits all approach is as inappropriate for bilingual students as it is for the English-speaking majority. A team of colleagues at School V works together in the first few weeks in order to get to know the student and to determine the best possible curriculum for him or her to follow.

The above research was presented to the school leadership team of School V in July 2007. Upon consideration of the options, the school leadership team abandoned plans to place most bilingual KS4 entrants in an EAL option for three hours per week, preferring to continue to integrate the majority of these students fully into the mainstream, providing additional and continuing support.

Having considered the various models, the school has delayed the implementation of the EAL pathway originally timetabled to begin in September 2007. This allows for a period of further research, including the opportunity to visit schools where similar models are working well, in order to begin in September 2008 a carefully planned, well-resourced and flexible course. During the school year 2007-2008, different models of in-class support will be piloted and students' and parents' views sought as to the most appropriate ways to meet the needs of bilingual students in the school.

The principal outcome of this research has been the increased awareness of senior colleagues at School W of the range of issues to be considered when planning for raised achievement of bilingual students. The work is on-going and the curriculum for newly arrived bilingual students in KS4 will need regular review to meet the needs of individual students in years to come.

A vocational college which offers a *Skills for Life* course for fifteen students from ten nationalities provides another example, from the college side, of the KS4-KS5 transition. This is a year's course but very much a roll-on, roll-off one with applications through the year. Course staff compile a detailed background profile of the student to ensure that participants are on the right course or at the right college. For the student the course provides ESOL, numeracy, maths, literacy, ICT, citizenship, access to counselling service, tutorials and leisure activities. ESOL, numeracy, maths, literacy and ICT are all at an appropriate level. Some of the ESOL is provided by in-filling existing Adult National Curriculum classes. Teaching support assistants are provided for mainstream classes.

This course provides a staging point between a small amount of time in secondary school aged 14-16 or arrival into the country at 16 plus and a vocational course at college where tutors may be apprehensive about enrolling students directly if their English is limited. How the college has endeavoured to build in flexibility for individual students is outlined here:

A mathematical language course caters for students:

- who have obtained a C at GCSE maths but want to achieve a higher grade

- who are in the highest GCSE group but have Adult National Curriculum Level 1 in English

- who are bored in a foundation GCSE maths group but frustrated in a higher group

In addition

- all the maths classes take place on one day so that students can move to different groups

- college has split mathematical language into two groups with the lower level continuing with the course for a whole year and the higher group moving into a GCSE support group after the planned six months

- vocational courses have language support

- college takes account of interruptions to courses particularly if interruptions happen in another country

- college provides accredited courses linked to the adult national curriculum as required by Adult Learning Inspectorate (ALI) but also monitors by providing appropriate informal learning and checking impact on learners

- college will consider changing format of life skills course to meet needs of different individuals in subsequent years

- college has tried to obtain travel and other grants from Ethnic Minority Achievement Service (EMA), refugee action group, Ruth Hayman Trust, Adult Learning Grants

- college has ensured that there are sets of course books in the library so that students don't have to purchase their own

- the entry requirement is that they don't speak English

- college encourages 80 per cent of students to do exams and enters students for Adult National Curriculum Level Entry 1

- college has tried to work with monolingual students who have been unsettled by the presence of a relatively large group of bilingual students, for example five out of six out of a class of fifteen. The monolingual students appear to be jealous of the high mathematical ability shown by the bilingual students and find it hard to believe that students from other countries can have better results than students coming through the English education system

- the complaints from monolingual students are expressed not as a direct complaint about bilingual students but in terms of noise in workshops and, paradoxically, reluctance of monolingual students to share their results openly and also answering questions before others have had chances to think about their own answers

- there is a recognition that equality and diversity and child protection systems need to be well embedded in college practices with induction for new staff

- two students from the Skills For Life programme are on the college students' committee and the co-ordinator is a college governor

- college reflects on cultural and religious needs. There is, for instance, a prayer room but during Ramadan no social place for Muslim students to meet each other without food

- the outcomes of the Skills for Life course can be measured qualitatively rather than quantitatively at the moment. The key outcome is integration across the college and a marked increase in confidence. It may also account for reducing depression in the case of unaccompanied asylum seekers. In the case of mathematics, mathematically minded students can enjoy lessons without waiting for language; perhaps otherwise they would wait for ever

- the collaborative focus in classes allows students to explain concepts or language to their partners or groups and rehearse their thinking for themselves

- embedded language materials are available for science and health and social care, beauty, engineering and other vocational subjects as college recognises that a level 2 in ESOL withers without use

- Cambridge International English Language Testing System (IELTS) is the pre-university course of choice. Staff have to stress its suitability for home as well as overseas students

It is vital that the careers service is involved and guidance is provided for students and their parents to understand the education system for post 16s as there is a tradition in many countries of education lasting until young people are 19 or 20 and some are surprised by the break at 16.

In another part of Hampshire, colleges, schools and the specialist EMA service are making links to ensure that students have as smooth a transition as possible from school inside or outside the country. These include plans to:

- provide part-time ESOL alongside school provision for under 16s so that they do not have to take a full year out of their academic or vocational 16-19 education

- carry out a survey of all transitions of 16 year olds and referrals of over 16s to ensure that there is appropriate placement and career service involvement for all students

- provide guidance for all ethnic minority 14-19 year olds and their families

- defer a place at college for a year for a young person needing more time at school to complete GCSEs

These are small steps in addressing language learning and teaching issues in the current 14-19 situation and it will be crucial to have appropriate provision in place when the 14-19 curriculum comes on stream from 2008.

There is clearly scope currently for building capacity within school improvement and more widely within children's services including 14-19 provision. The picture is still patchy but gradually the pieces are forming a coherent whole so that, no matter where a bilingual learner is found in the county, there will be joined up approaches to their educational provision.

3

Professional development and the developing role of teaching assistants in relation to isolated EAL learners

Anwen Foy

Reflections on classroom assistants' training

Teaching assistants (TAs) have a long history of supporting pupils with English as an Additional Language (EAL) in schools with isolated learners. In many parts of the country they continue to deliver the bulk of the support, but they are increasingly taking on enhanced roles in this area. This chapter will explore some of the different ways in which TAs contribute to EAL practice and provision, and will also identify practical ways in which specialist training can empower TAs to make a real difference to bilingual learners at their schools.

In the 1980s and early 1990s, TAs were often the first port of call when new arrivals came through the school doors. In the absence of specialist training, limited (if any) local authority support services or sources of expertise in schools with isolated learners, TAs found themselves operating alone, delivering a varied programme of support. This ranged from the use of phonically based reading schemes and teaching basic survival English to grammar based exercises more commonly found in English as a Foreign Language (EFL) classes. Much of this support was delivered outside the classroom on a withdrawal basis, without very much reference to the curriculum or to pupils' first language and prior knowledge. Many TAs were inventive and creative in sourcing and producing resources for pupils new to English, whilst others went back to basics – for example, using materials designed for much younger learners, focusing on colours, numbers, or forming basic decontextualised sentences.

These types of practices prevailed for a variety of reasons. Many schools felt (and some still do) that pupils new to English should be provided with basic English before being integrated into class. Others may have felt disempowered by lack of knowledge about EAL and simply provided extra person power to support pupils. In some schools, there was a perception of EAL learners as a problem whose needs should be met by other people or outside services rather than being seen as a whole school responsibility. The reality in isolated areas was that other people or services simply did not exist and many TAs therefore shouldered responsibility for teaching English to new arrivals as best they could.

Although many schools responded by making best use of the resources they had available, there were obvious flaws in some of the approaches adopted. Regarding pupils with EAL as a whole school responsibility is a recurrent theme in much of the evidence from research into current good EAL practice (QCA, 2000; Hall, 1995; DfES, 2004a). Having a named designated manager with appropriate skills, knowledge and expertise, who can co-ordinate support and oversee ethnic minority achievement (including EAL) in a whole school context provides positive benefits for pupils, staff and parents.

Practitioners are also now more aware that there are limitations to withdrawing pupils with EAL for basic survival English as a language acquisition strategy. This is because conversational fluency and the type of language needed to survive generally develop quite rapidly regardless of interventions when pupils are learning alongside their peers and interacting with them.

Conversely, the subject specific, more academic language of the curriculum often requires support and intervention for pupils with EAL to acquire it effectively. This is the kind of language that can open doors for pupils into higher levels of academic attainment and so is more likely to have an impact on life chances. It is therefore an area where support may be more usefully targeted.

We should not lose sight of the fact that pupils with EAL arrive at school with a variety of skills and knowledge, and do not necessarily have to pass a particular threshold in English in order to be included in a classroom context and learn curriculum content. For example, after watching a video about earthquakes, a new arrival could create and label a diagram (in their preferred language) to explain this phenomenon, perhaps drawing on prior knowledge, without having developed a particular level of English first. Ofsted argue that:

> ...it is 'unnecessary, indeed unhelpful, to separate language and content learning, the majority of EAL teaching should take place within the mainstream and across the curriculum. (Ofsted, 2001 p17)

It is still the case that TAs are supporting pupils with EAL but in Hampshire at least, the general picture is different from that described earlier and continues to evolve and change. We are currently in a transitional phase in terms of TA roles, careers and professional development structures. The changing roles of TAs in relation to EAL reflect this. In addition to delivering the support, TAs (or teams of TAs) are now more likely to take on increased responsibility and co-ordinate provision for EAL learners at their school. The following vignette is by a TA who has been a teacher of English as a foreign language in other employment. It illustrates some of the changing roles of TAs.

The extracts for this journal are taken from the secondary school where I am employed as an EAL teaching assistant. The theme focuses on the issues for support, inclusion of EAL students in the classroom and withdrawal of students or lesson support outside the class.

In the role of teaching assistant it is possible to get an overall perspective of the classroom in relation to how the students are receiving and comprehending the information that is being taught to them.

The reflective descriptions revolve mainly around support for the EAL student where interaction between myself and the learners helps to foster understanding and lesson objectives.

An important factor to point out is that my job is part-time so I need to be flexible, in the sense that I go into classes and support students for whom assistance is most needed; but from time to time they can be the learners with stronger English ability as well as the ones with the weakest. On top of this, there is no specific

---

timetable unlike that of the normal teaching assistants for me to follow so I am not necessarily supporting the same students in the same subjects every week.

I worked with a Year 8 student from Portugal with weak English language skills last year. The support for her was a combination of being in class and withdrawal. In a history lesson the students were studying the English Civil War and its aftermath; for this they were going to watch a video depicting the execution of Charles 1. The teacher explained to the students that they needed to make observations (with bullet points) with a view to writing a diary for homework describing the death of Charles 1 from either a Parliamentarian or a Royalist point of view.

The student I was supporting didn't exactly grasp the lesson's objectives; she was able to distinguish some words from the teacher's explanation, but she wasn't sure about the concept of writing a diary – taking the view of one side or the other.

As the teacher explained the lesson's objectives orally, I talked through with the student what the teacher wanted her to do. I briefly discussed events leading up to the execution of Charles 1 and gave her some examples of the observations she would need to look out for to write the bullet points.

During the video I wrote down some bullet points as examples to prompt the student while discussing key parts of the clip with her for possible inclusion in the diary she would have to write. At the end of the video clip, the teacher elicited responses from the students for a list of bullet points to be written on the board which the student duly wrote in her book.

I arranged to work with her in afternoon tutor time and go through the bullet points, and then help her with the diary extract. In the library we discussed the lesson and the bullet points that had been written down. We talked about the Royalists and Parliamentarians using a text book for reference and learning source to encourage verbal observations.

We talked about the concept of a diary – this having to be fully understood, especially as it would have to be written in the past tense. The idea was then presented of her putting herself in the position of being either a Royalist or a Parliamentarian – what would she have been? We discussed these hypothetical concepts and she came to the conclusion that she would have been a Parliamentarian.

I employed guided writing techniques in the shape of starter sentences that were the result of our discussions about what would be the contents of the diary this enabled writing targets to be addressed through this interactive approach (DfES, 2002a).

The objectives that were set out in the class and the way they were presented to the students revolved around the assumption that an EAL learner would naturally focus on and comprehend the input they were receiving. The instructions were totally oral and delivered in a colloquial manner that went far over the top of the student's head.

From the teacher's point of view there seemed to be the need to press on with the class and to make sure that all of the lesson's objectives would be achieved. The student appeared unsure what was expected of her. It might have been possible to write some examples on the board, with ideas from the students, to enforce the oral instructions to the class. It might have been possible to ask the EAL student for an easy sentence initially.

As the class has no other Portuguese speakers the use of first language as additional support is not forthcoming as a means to accelerate learning, where pairs or groups of students who share the same language can rehearse responses in their mother tongue before engaging in English.

The point I tried to get across, however, was the need to place the EAL learner among some good role model students. In this way these students could possibly enhance the linguistic capability of the EAL pupil through interactive talk between them and so increase the Portuguese learner's literacy skills.

It became evident in a later class that a particular small group assignment epitomised some of these linguistic points where the students through a movie making task needed to collaborate on suggestions and ideas; these interactive exchanges characterised the advantages of group work where the unconfident learner feels less intimidated than in the teacher centred learning environment. At the end of the class I passed on the positive outcomes of the task to the teacher, expressing these linguistic benefits from the point of view of the learner, which seemed to fall on more receptive ears.

In another lesson, this time geography, on Antarctica, four learners understood the objectives of the lesson but didn't use key words like the monolingual learners in the class. They wrote down notes using vocabulary that reflected their spoken use of English. One of the students said she understood most of the key words but when I asked her to explain, she didn't know, or her description was unrelated to the subject context.

I wrote down the key words with explanations in the context of the subject so that the students were able to use these along with drawings and physical gestures to help with their writing. I arranged a support lesson in an afternoon tutor time to go over the words in relation to the class topic and the idea that words in a different context can have other meanings.

From the feedback I gave the teacher at the end of the class, I made a point of emphasising the need to be aware of words used to express differing concepts. Her reaction was sympathetic and appreciative. As Cooke and Pike (2000) wrote 'teachers do need to recognise what vocabulary, structures and discourse features make comprehension more difficult and mediate these demands in light of analysis'.

The support, therefore, that I am able to give as a teaching assistant reflects a bridging role between myself, the student and the teacher. What I feel, however, is for that role to be more effective there needs to be a greater platform for communication with the teacher and myself to bring about more effective planning that can enhance learning. With the means to employ methods to plan ahead, the objective of giving the EAL student the maximum amount of support possible can be realised.

The development of specialist training for teaching assistants

Training and development for teachers has been a focus for a long time but in the past other school staff have often been neglected. In 2002, the DfES piloted induction training for teaching assistants in response to clear evidence of lack of training and development opportunities. Further developments have included national guidance containing model job profiles, employment good practice, and advice on the development of school support staff, which was agreed by the National Joint Council for local government services. This provided useful guidance on progression routes (skills and qualifications) for TAs and further clarification of the different aspects of their role.

In Hampshire, the DfES *English as an additional language: induction training for teaching assistants in primary and secondary schools.* (2004a) was delivered by the Ethnic Minority Achievement Service (EMAS) to over 200 TAs during the first year. The positive response reflected the increased involvement at a local level, of TAs in EAL. At the same time, training for teachers attracted a much poorer response. TAs locally, were fast overtaking teachers in terms of their skills and knowledge about EAL issues.

In 2004, an opportunity arose to develop specialist accredited training in EAL for TAs in the authority, in partnership with Portsmouth EMAS and the University of Portsmouth. There had already been a long history of training for bilingual assistants in Hampshire, by virtue of a specialist course originally developed by a forward thinking member of the Portsmouth EMAS team. This evolved into SEAL – Supporting English as an Additional Language – a specialist course for teaching assistants, piloted and run in Hampshire and Portsmouth. This was particularly timely in Hampshire, as it met the needs of a growing number of schools in which TAs had taken on the co-ordination of EAL and fuller responsibility for this area.

Co-ordination of EAL by teaching assistants has both advantages and disadvantages as an approach. This is particularly true in a context with isolated learners. Levels of expertise in this field may be very variable; access to colleagues with subject knowledge in EAL may be harder to find. Styles of provision and support may differ greatly from school to school and there may be ambiguity in relation to roles and responsibility towards pupils with EAL. Families may be isolated without access to the community support or the multilingual services that are more likely to exist in multi-ethnic areas. However, there may also be greater flexibility and open mindedness in the absence of any established approaches of practices to support EAL learners.

On the positive side, modern day teaching assistants are increasingly multi talented and often have a complex role involving a multitude of different tasks and duties. Enhanced training opportunities through the National Strategies, and rapidly changing roles as a result of Workforce Remodelling, have contributed to career minded TAs who are capable of fulfilling a whole school responsibility such as EAL. Some schools recognise that an enhanced role in EAL could offer career progression for talented TAs or would sit alongside HLTA (Higher Level Teaching Assistant) status very comfortably.

Many TAs have varied life experiences which provide skills that are particularly useful in the field of EAL. For example, they may have lived, worked and taught abroad. Some have English as a Foreign Language (EFL) teaching experience, but do not have Qualified Teacher Status. Despite differences in ideology between EFL and EAL (for instance the emphasis placed on the target language in EFL and the emphasis on valuing and using first language for learning in EAL), these TAs may have a well developed knowledge of language and a keen interest and enthusiasm for using their skills in mainstream settings. Some TAs may be bilingual themselves, or show an aptitude for supporting pupils with EAL.

On an operational level, schools with relatively low numbers of pupils with EAL may feel that having a TA as co-ordinator is the most viable option and one which will best support both pupils and teachers. TAs can be deployed more flexibly than teachers. They often have an opportunity to see pupils in a range of contexts and are well placed to identify the most effective support strategies for both individuals and groups. Being amongst the pupils often makes TAs more approachable than teachers to pupils with EAL who may otherwise feel very isolated. There are, there-fore, certain advantages in the less formal relationships TAs are able to form with pupils. Some EAL learners may relate better to someone in this type of role. A dual role encompassing co-ordination and delivery of sup-port has certain advantages in this respect. However, it can rapidly be-come an unmanageable workload as the numbers of EAL learners rise, when they have other responsibilities.

Whilst there are undoubtedly advantages, there are also significant chal-lenges to be overcome in assigning responsibility for EAL to a teaching assistant. It can lead schools to regard EAL solely as the responsibility of dedicated support staff rather than a whole school responsibility re-quiring a strategic approach. A by product of this is the marginalisation of EAL as an issue and thus the – albeit unintentional – marginalisation of EAL learners within the school. This situation is exacerbated where senior leaders are new to EAL themselves and may wish to introduce or impose models of support based on withdrawal rather than inclusion. This can increase isolation for TAs, pupils and their families.

A questionnaire sent out to some of the earliest course participants in-cluded the question *How is responsibility for EAL shared within your school?* This provided some interesting responses. One respondent replied that 'in theory EAL should be the responsibility of all' which sug-gests that it may be a different matter in practice. Other respondents replied that it was shared amongst TAs, or the class teacher and TA's joint responsibility, or it was not anyone's main responsibility. Only one res-pondent replied that it was a whole school responsibility. This suggests that, in schools with isolated learners, EAL can be perceived as an indivi-dual pupil issue rather than an issue requiring a whole school strategic response. It also suggests a tendency towards a more *ad hoc*, reactive approach to EAL. It becomes an issue only when there are new pupils requiring support. The TA co-ordinator is at the mercy of these fluctuations.

There will also be ethical concerns, where TAs may be required to do the job of a teacher or co-ordinator without the salary to match. For some, the burden of this role may become overwhelming, particularly where numbers of EAL learners rise unpredictably. In schools with isolated EAL learners, isolation can quickly spread to TAs who are co-ordinating EAL provision, unless there is sufficient support from colleagues and senior management at the school. This may be particularly true in cases where TAs have found themselves thrust into this role by simply expressing an interest in this field.

A further concern is that TAs do not always have a strong voice in their school and may struggle to influence teaching colleagues. This may be particularly the case in relation to issues such as assessment, teaching strategies, setting and grouping of pupils with EAL, which have traditionally always been in the domain of teachers. For example, it is a very confident and knowledgeable TA who asks an experienced teacher why she has placed an able Polish new arrival in the bottom set rather than with good English role models. In relation to the use of standardised tests on entry into school, one course participant observed with frustration that:

> when it comes to putting the students into the correct grouping teachers look at the result of the test and will automatically assume that they need to be placed into lower groups rather than the higher ones. It is hard to convince the teachers that the students are able to produce the higher standards without the proof of what they are capable of doing.

When the TA is the sole expert in EAL in the school, this situation can pose even more of a challenge. Concerns of this nature need to be weighed up carefully by schools who are considering appointing a TA co-ordinator for EAL in their setting.

Supporting English as an Additional Language

In Hampshire, the SEAL course endeavoured to address some of these issues and build in support for TAs facing the particular challenges of working with isolated learners. Some of the ways in which this was achieved are described below and were developed jointly by the Portsmouth and Hampshire training teams.

Collaborating with colleagues

An emphasis was placed on collaborating with colleagues and disseminating what course participants had learnt in order to reduce feelings of isolation as well as begin to build capacity within the school. For example, assessment tasks focused TAs on the need to undertake joint planning of a task, discuss ideas in staff meetings, obtain feedback on materials produced, share work in the classroom and model different approaches. Tasks were worded accordingly as shown in these examples.

- work with a colleague to provide a draft....
- in consultation with class/subject teacher, plan....
- in co-operation with the class/subject teacher, identify...
- share your findings with a colleague/s....
- create a draft document for consultation with the whole staff...
- carry out some observations of pupil A. Feed back what you have observed to....

One course participant planned a task and resource with a teacher who initially was sceptical about the value of more collaborative approaches in the classroom. Following the joint trial of the resource in the classroom, the teacher commented that the activity had 'worked very well and made significant improvement to the knowledge of EAL students that I teach.'

A similar task provided an opportunity for a different TA to raise teacher expectations for EAL learners in a Geography class. Initially sceptical about the ability of EAL learners to access concepts and language relating to earthquakes, the support provided for language acquisition through a collaborative resource meant that by the end of the activity, this teacher had to eat her words! Both TAs were able to impact on the perceptions and attitudes of teaching colleagues through modelling resources and activities pitched at an appropriately challenging level. The second TA was also able to use this situation to challenge pupil groupings within the class. Thus, one successful method of finding a voice is to lead by example. This helps to build credibility and trust with colleagues who may previously have been sceptical or ignorant about the skills and talents of TAs at their school

Speaking with conviction

As part of the ongoing assessment, course participants were asked to prepare and deliver a series of presentations to their fellow students. For many, this was a new and nerve-wracking experience. Few had experience of this (in an adult context at least) or had ever used any kind of audio visual equipment to support their input. There were, however, many positive spin offs, not least, a tangible improvement in TAs' self confidence and their ability to speak with conviction. This was probably due to a combination of increased subject knowledge and an enhancement of public speaking skills. This proved invaluable in being able to disseminate learning and more broadly to develop a professional role and voice within the school. At the end of the course, one TA prefaced a comment with 'I can't believe I'm saying this' before stating that one of the most valuable aspects of the course had been the requirement to plan and deliver presentations. She had found that she had developed a great deal more confidence to talk to others and make her views known. This view was echoed by others on the course.

Using technology to disseminate ideas and information

Advances in technology in schools can provide further non-threatening opportunities to establish a professional voice at a school. Many TAs found it useful to disseminate learning from the course in a targeted way, using the school intranet. In fact, many TAs became sensitised to the ways in which they needed to put information across so that it was palatable and more manageable for teaching colleagues in the light of busy workloads.

Pupil voice

Setting tasks which require TAs to engage views of pupils and presenting some of these views to colleagues can provide powerful evidence for the need to change practice in a particular area. For example, when compiling classroom support strategies to share with colleagues at the school, several TAs sought the views of EAL learners to try to find out what made the difference to them when they were new to English. This shed light on the experience of being a new arrival in that particular school. One TA found that a Russian pupil had felt very isolated and left out, and made no friends for an entire year. The TA said that it:

> ...opened my eyes a lot – I didn't realise how much EAL students are discriminated against in a way. I don't know if the school's not thought of it. That's something that [colleague] and I will be able to do [something] about.

Setting clear expectations

A further way to reduce possible isolation for TAs was to build in a pre-paration period for discussing course requirements with school managers. An agreement form, detailing what was to be provided by the course, and what needed to be provided by the school, was found to be a useful way of supporting TAs once they had started their course. For example, it was possible to discuss the need to

- release TA for the course...

- provide a critical friend for informal discussions/to act as a sounding board for ideas...

- offer additional study time if possible

- facilitate opportunities for dissemination

Choosing a colleague from within the school, to act as a critical friend for each course participant, provided a means of providing moral support, helping with problem solving and facilitating access to people or re-sources. Critical friends ranged from another TA, a line manager, a teaching colleague, head teacher, SENCO or any member of staff able to support students in the ways described.

Conclusions

Co-ordinating EAL as a Teaching Assistant clearly poses huge challenges, particularly for those working in isolated contexts. Schools have variable levels of knowledge and expertise, EAL may be viewed as outside the remit of mainstream teachers, and TAs may meet a varied response to any changes in their role. However, with a supportive school leadership team and an inclusive ethos, some TAs have undoubtedly been able to in-fluence teaching colleagues and help to change the way in which EAL is viewed. Training providers need to take account of the context in which participants work and build in support to help overcome barriers – the very real barriers that many TAs may face in this new and developing role.

Anwen Foy is the deputy team leader with the Hampshire Ethnic Minority Achievement Service. She has led a range of professional development initiatives across the county, aimed to raise capacity and support schools with isolated bilingual learners in particular.

4

Assessing isolated bilingual learners

Judith Howard

This chapter offers guidance on the initial assessment of isolated pupils arriving in a school. It is specifically aimed at schools that have limited experience of new arrivals from other countries or cultural backgrounds and those whose pupils and families may be isolated in the local community.

Guidance on assessment of new arrivals, including isolated children, is now available in various forms, including publications from the DfES and DCSF particularly the *Primary and Secondary Strategies*, with specific reference to the *New Arrivals Excellence Programme* (DfES and DCFS, 2007) guidance. How to prepare, how to go about assessment and why assessment is so important for the ongoing monitoring of progress of the child will all be discussed.

The response of schools unfamiliar with new arrivals from other countries can range from mild consternation to panic. Very often teachers are fearful; they don't know what to expect and they feel they will not be able to meet the needs of the child. Preparation is a wonderful thing. Although a head teacher may feel that preparation for a relatively rare event is not a priority, these situations are becoming more and more common for all schools and a degree of preparation can make a tremendous difference to the welcoming of a family into the school community.

The term child will be used in this chapter, in relation to all key stages, in order to emphasise not only the child's position as a pupil in school and a learner of English, but also the whole child beginning a new life in different circumstances.

Preparation

What can be put in place in terms of preparation? Two main areas of preparation could be considered here – a more general whole school approach to preparation, and preparation for an imminent new arrival.

In broad terms schools could consider:

- policy – for example in terms of race equality, equal opportunities or induction of pupils with English as an Additional Language (EAL)

- staff training for teachers, teaching assistants, administrative staff

- procedures in the event of a new arrival being admitted

Although policy is not considered in any detail here, it is important to say that all policies could include consideration of a child from an ethnic minority, including a potential new arrival in school. The policy on assessment therefore might include consideration of some of the issues relating to assessment of a new arrival.

Training is vital. Training could be aimed at one or two members of staff, perhaps an interested teacher and teaching assistant, who would then carry forward and maintain that knowledge and be able to disseminate it when the situation arises.

This school-based trained person would have basic awareness of issues and would know what to do next and where to access support. There are courses available, introductory or more in depth, such as the courses running in Hampshire at the moment – Supporting English as an Additional Language (SEAL) and Teaching English as an Additional Language (TEAL) and induction training for teaching assistants. The important thing is that a member of staff could be called on in the event of a newly arrived child in school.

What general information could be held by this member of staff?

- is there a local ethnic minority achievement (EMA) service? Contact numbers and information

- if not, are there any other local contacts that could be of help, for example schools in the vicinity which may have more experience?

- are there any staff who have any experience or interest in the area of EAL?

- are there any staff who speak other languages?

- what translation services are available? Contact numbers and information

- are there any resources available, for example dual language materials or information on different cultural backgrounds?

Another element of forward planning is to consider the awareness of administrative staff. The administrative staff are likely to be the first contact for the family, carrying the responsibility for the first impression of the school on their shoulders. They need to be ready for parents and children who have limited ability to communicate in English and who, additionally, may have little idea of the educational system in this country or style of education in the classroom. Families may have come from a country where children begin school at a different age so their younger children may be coming into a formal school setting for the first time.

For these reasons, administrative staff need to adopt a positive approach. They need basic awareness of the possible feelings of the family – what is it like to try to get your child into a school in an educational system which you don't fully understand yet, when you feel you may not be able to explain yourself fully and clearly, when you are worried that your child will feel isolated and friendless, when you are still coping with your own shock at being in a new environment and with your extended family far away? Of course, staff will not have detailed knowledge of each family's background and circumstances but they can develop empathy by considering those issues.

Simple steps to welcome a child or family in school can be taken without a huge investment of time. Information is often readily available in terms of language, culture and translation. A welcoming ethos in school is often largely dependent on the way staff and pupils react to the new arrival, their expressions, their attitudes.

Simple measures could be considered, such as a welcome poster in the reception area that includes the child's language. Perhaps the information given to families in the school handbook needs to be considered in terms of accessibility to families whose first language is not English. Perhaps there is an opportunity for translation of key documents or for verbal explanation through the first language, remembering that the school environment and system of education may be outside any previous experience of the child or family.

Additionally, it is helpful to find out some basic details about the cultural background of the family, in particular anything that might affect the child's settling in. Information about cultural backgrounds and languages is easily available, and vital in order to be able to understand a little of what the family is adapting to. Additionally, there may be time to acquire dual language materials in the child's language or to provide simple glossaries. At the same time it is important for administrative staff to record children's ethnic code, language(s) and religion for ethnic monitoring.

For the pupils in an established class, the arrival of another pupil who does not share the language of the class can be a fascinating experience. The reaction of a class to a new arrival is one of the most important early experiences for the new arrival. Preparation of the class, particularly in terms of empathy and understanding as to how it might feel to arrive in a country where you may be isolated and unable to communicate freely, can have an enormous impact. A short lesson in a language unknown to the class can be an eye opening experience for both pupils and staff and can help develop empathy. The simple step of learning how to say hello and goodbye in the new language can break so many barriers. It may also be possible to gather translations of some useful statements or questions for the use of the child and the teacher, survival language relating to everyday needs.

The initial assessment

The family has arrived! They have crossed the threshold and have been assisted in filling in the admission forms and have been shown around by a welcoming member of staff.

In a well-prepared school, a named school contact could be introduced to the family who would have an understanding of some of the issues facing the child, school and family. At this point, this school contact could in turn contact appropriate agencies such as an EMA service or would be able to call on translation and interpreting services already researched and available. It may be that an EMA service would be able to provide an initial assessment of the child or provide a bilingual assistant so that further assessment in the first language can take place.

How can a child be assessed if they speak little English? What can be assessed, especially if a bilingual assistant is not available? Do we simply require an assessment of English?

It is always worth reminding ourselves that we are considering a whole person not simply a child who does not speak English. This child has usually had experience of an educational system before arriving in this country. They have their own strengths and weaknesses, likes and dislikes, opinions, knowledge of maths, science and other areas of the curriculum. They have their own social skills, friendship groups, and position in a family, their own attitude to teachers and other adults. Of course they have. But sometimes this is overshadowed by the simple fact that they can't yet communicate effectively in English.

Considering the whole child then, we need to take into account all that the child has to offer and not just their ability in English. We need actively to find out about the child's previous educational experiences and knowledge so that they can be valued and built upon. We need to know as much as possible about the child's strengths in order to sustain self esteem at a time when this can be very vulnerable.

So who could be involved in this initial assessment? Certainly the child, but also the parents, if possible a bilingual assistant, a trained school-based member of staff or alternatively a member of an EMA service working in conjunction with the class teacher.

This initial assessment might include:

- an assessment of the child's development in the first language

- gathering information about the child's previous schooling, from reports, from parents and the child

- gathering information about the child eg likes and dislikes, feelings about being here

- an assessment of the child's health, any difficulties with hearing or sight

- background information on the family, family circumstances, any evidence of trauma

- general cultural background information

- information on the first language and how it works, its script

- and last, but not least, an assessment of the child's use of English and knowledge of the parents' use of English

One response to this might be, why do we need to know all this about a child? Can it be intrusive? How does it affect how the child will cope in the classroom or learn English?

Consideration of the whole child can help schools offer support, not only in development of English, but in settling into a new environment, having access to the curriculum and making friends. It can help involve parents, help staff understand the child as an individual and help them to tap into strengths and abilities.

All of this will have an impact on the child's self esteem and sense of wellbeing. A relaxed and happy child will make friends more easily and therefore be in a better position to acquire English both in lessons and in interaction with other children and adults in school. This child is not the same as any other child arriving in school. I, myself moved to another part of the country when I was in the middle of the school year and it was a memorable experience – differences between my old school and my new school, making new friends in an established class, teasing because of my accent, and difficulties in adjusting. But what I did know was the nature of school life in this country and the language of communication with my new peers. A newly arrived child from another country has many more hurdles to overcome and this should be acknowledged and respected in the spirit of *Every Child Matters* (DfES, 2004b).

How can parents contribute to the assessment process? Parents can offer valuable information about the educational background of the child. This could include the previous school curriculum, school systems, starting age at schools, languages used in school, styles of teaching and learning, attitudes to education, homework, discipline and so on. The parents can also give specific information about their own child's strengths and weaknesses, social skills, health issues and development of first language. The school can find out about the parents' expectations, any concerns they may have, their understanding of the UK school system. If the parents are given an opportunity to meet staff in these early stages, it can avoid many misunderstandings and encourage the parents to feel a part of their child's education. It is also an opportunity to help the parents themselves settle into the community and perhaps be made aware of any support for them in the local area. With the additional support of bilingual assistants, this information sharing can be enhanced to a much higher level and will help parents feel valued and welcomed by the school and less isolated in the community.

Having all this information can help enormously in seeing the child within the context of family and community, which will in turn provide a more effective assessment.

What is involved in this initial assessment? Before considering this, it is important to choose an appropriate time to assess a newly arrived child. Being responsive to the individual's need for a settling in period, allowing the child enough time to feel comfortable and balancing this with the need for an early assessment will provide a better quality of assessment. At this stage an informal talk with the child can assist the settling in process. It is also an opportunity to find out further information from the child's perspective. A quiet time set aside without interruption or noise can be an opportunity for the child to express their feelings about their new situation.

In my experience of talking with children, even those who speak very little or no English are able to express their feelings to an extent, with the help of gesture or visual support. And it is an excellent opportunity to find out how to pronounce the child's name correctly!

Adapting or simplifying language so that it can be more easily understood for someone with limited English is a skill that can be developed over time but a friendly manner and genuine interest are attributes that can enable communication to take place even in these early stages. Many children have encountered a few words of English, sufficient to facilitate these early conversations but even children with no English can appreciate the time and interest given to them. Using visuals relating to school together with visuals relating to facial expression can result in information on likes and dislikes, preferred subjects, feelings about breaks. With just a little English, a lot of information can be gained about the child's assessment of their own strengths and weaknesses, likes and dislikes, feelings about school/peers and so on.

A large part of an initial assessment is actually observation, to include:

- observation outside the classroom (in the playground, at lunch-time, interaction with peers)

- observation in the classroom (in group work, individual work, whole class work, interaction with peers)

The playground and break times are important places to observe the child as these times can be some of the most difficult for a new arrival. Are the other children inviting the new arrival to join them? Is the child standing apart? Are the lunchtime supervisors aware of the fact that the child may have limited English language skills and feel isolated?

Observation in the classroom could consider:

- is the child appropriately placed in the class?

- does the child have access to any support eg visual support for a story or clear access to an interactive whiteboard?

- does the child seem to switch off after a short time?

- does the child appear to have any sensory difficulties?

In groups or individual work:

- how does the child interact with peers?

- what kind of social skills does the child have?

- is the child able to access or participate in the curriculum with support?

- does the child show understanding of what teachers/peers are saying?

- is the child able to ask for help?

- does the child appear relaxed and at ease in the classroom?

- does the child appear familiar with the types of task/activity/area of the curriculum?

In some areas of Hampshire, where there have been large numbers of new arrivals from a particular country, a form of self-profiling has been developed. Children are asked to consider questions about their needs, hopes, previous educational experiences, knowledge of English and feelings about their new environment. A bilingual assistant is on hand to support the children who are encouraged to complete their profiling forms in any language in which they are literate. Children are able to speak to the bilingual assistant individually, certainly if they feel unable to cope with the literacy demands of the profiling, and they are encouraged to inform the bilingual assistant of what support they feel they might need. The bilingual assistant is then able to provide feedback on the children and make recommendations for individual children. Self assessment is a valuable tool for all children, certainly in terms of Assessment for Learning, but the concept of self assessment may be quite alien to some new arrivals in terms of previous educational experience.

A significant part of an early assessment is of course considering the child's use of English. What should we consider in this respect?

Speaking and listening
In terms of speaking and listening, we can note whether the child:

- is responding in one word answers

- is responding in short phrases

- is responding in more extended utterances

- is expressing him/herself mainly through gesture or demonstration

- is showing evidence of understanding (eg following instructions)

- is confident in their attitude to attempting English

For children whose level of English is more advanced, we can note whether the child can:

- use English in a fluent way

- use English fluently but with a different pronunciation

- use verbs and tenses

- use appropriate word order

- use less familiar vocabulary

- use articles, prepositions and other parts of speech

Pronunciation is an interesting consideration. Sometimes a different style of spoken English can mislead school staff into thinking that the family/child does not have a good level of English as they may have difficulty in making themselves understood. Often this is a hurdle for both families and schools as both adjust to the other's style of spoken English. This can be very demoralising for a family coming from an environment where English is a part of everyday life, yet finding they cannot be understood easily in the local area.

If a child is arriving from, for example, Southern India, it is valuable to look into the conventions of the language spoken. Are there verb tenses? Are there articles? Is the word order different from English? What is the script/alphabet/orientation of writing? Are the sounds different from English sounds? How are questions formed? Even those few facts can give enormous insight into the child's acquisition of English. Many languages have a different system of tenses, articles, prepositions. Just by knowing this, we can partly predict which areas of English might be more difficult for that child. A child without a similar tense structure in their own language will need time to acquire this new concept. On the other hand, a child who has a similar word order for prepositions will find that particular concept easier.

Why is it important to look at the features of language? For me, the answer is because it is fascinating! To be more specific:

- it can affect the child's acquisition of English

- it can help show the learning road that the child is on

- it can give us evidence of progress in English

- it helps teachers and teaching assistants to understand what is going on in the child's mind

The fact that many children acquire, for example, the past tense in English in a similar way to our first language acquisition of the past tense is both fascinating and also very commonsensical. Our newly arrived child may begin with little idea of how to express the past tense. They will hear people using different forms of a verb eg want/wanted. They will notice that sometimes the verb changes completely, eg: go/went, see/saw. They may experiment with verbs, using words such as 'bringed', eventually acquiring the correct use of the tense through repeated exposure to the correct form in context. I am not suggesting that a grammar lesson is needed for young children, but simply that acquisition takes time, is a process, needs a context and is a part of everyday access to the curriculum.

Reading

What about reading? How can that be assessed? If a child cannot read in English, is it possible to assess a child who is reading in their first language?

Although we may not get a full picture of the child's ability, we can certainly have an impression of the child's fluency and confidence in reading, familiarity with and enjoyment of books, attitude to reading. As already mentioned, there are many dual language materials available now in a range of languages. It might be possible to choose reading material from the child's own cultural background, possibly a familiar story, certainly at an age appropriate level for the child in terms of content. Reading with a bilingual assistant will provide information on the child's reading in much greater depth, in terms of accuracy, expression and specific skills. Nevertheless, valuable assessment information can be gained even without being able to understand the language of the child.

In assessing a child's reading in English, it is important to find text that is age appropriate. It can be very demoralising to be asked to read a book obviously aimed at a much younger child.

When reading English, the child will provide information on their knowledge of sounds/letters/script and the decoding process. They may impress you with their ability to decode. However some children are excellent at decoding English text but are completely unable to access meaning. I know myself how that is possible. I am Welsh and grew up with Welsh text around me, singing and reciting in Welsh, but I can't speak Welsh. I can read text quite effectively and people often expect me to know what I am talking about from my confidence in reading, but in reality only the occasional word is accessible to me. The general gist can often completely escape me – unless I have some visuals!

In reading aloud, a child can show which sounds they are having difficulty with, perhaps problems distinguishing vowel sounds, or using consonant clusters, or perhaps using sounds unknown in the first language. A child may also exhibit what type of system they have used to learn to read – do they sound words out? Do they spell words out? Do they look at the word as a whole? How do they approach unfamiliar vocabulary?

Writing

Similarly, when assessing writing, it is surprising how much information can be gained from assessing a piece of writing in a language unfamiliar to the assessor.

Imagine being invited to write something and then told that you have to write it in Bengali or Spanish or Russian. I personally would prefer to try in Spanish as at least I share my letter forms and alphabet to a large extent with Spanish. Imagine the result of your effort. I might feel humiliated but also anxious to show that I could write much better in my own language.

When assessing a child's writing, there is so much to gain from looking at an example of writing in the first language, even if we can't understand it. In a similar way to reading, we can gain information on the child's approach to writing – confident, fluent, hesitant, painstaking, with or without frequent crossing out, with or without punctuation? What script is used? What is the orientation of the writing? A bilingual assistant would be able to go much further and discuss expression, sentence construction, syntax, spelling, but again we can gain valuable information without understanding the language.

Assessing a child's writing in English can also provide information about where the child is in terms of acquiring English. Some of the considerations could be, is the child:

- able to form letters correctly?

- aware of punctuation?

- able to spell/recognise letter/sound relationships?

- able to construct a sentence?

- able to use a variety of tenses?

- able to express meaning effectively?

Here is a short extract from a piece of narrative written by a Chinese pupil:

> When I get ready to step on an ice I felt so scared because I haven't skate on an ice for nearly two years, so I might be not able to skate. And if I skate I have to get used to it so that I don't reliys that I'm going to fell over. I holded on my friend a bit tight and he was going fast. I skated with my teacher at the first time at that year and then I skated with her the second time and at the third time I made her and me fell.

There are two ways of looking at the extract: one is to see a range of errors; one is to see it as evidence showing progression in English.

When I see the word 'holded', I recognise that the child has discovered that past tenses can be formed by adding 'ed'. As in first language acquisition, the child may be applying the rule incorrectly but the evidence is there that the rule is being acquired. I might add that, as the child comes from a language background that does not have tenses in the same way as English, she is doing remarkably well in her acquisition of the structure of not just one but several tenses.

In the use of articles, I could say 'This child does not understand the use of definite and indefinite articles'. Or I could say, 'This child does not have articles in her first language, but she is beginning to try to use them and has done so appropriately on a number of occasions' (a very difficult thing for anyone to do). This shows progress.

If we have a little knowledge of the conventions of a child's first language, it enables us to recognise when developments are taking place and to recognise them as progress.

The QCA have in recent years developed a series of steps – *A Language in Common: assessing English as an additional language,* (QCA, 2000), recommended by the DCFS for use with learners of EAL above Foundation stage. These Step Descriptors show development in English before a child reaches Level 2 of the National Curriculum. The emphasis behind these steps is to focus on what the child *can* do rather than what a child *cannot* do: instead of classifying the child as 'pre level 1', the descriptors show the amount of progress that can be made in those early stages. The QCA Step Descriptors are specifically aimed at children with EAL and they provide teachers with a tool, in national use, that is clearly linked with the National Curriculum.

One of the most important uses of these early descriptors is in terms of a formative assessment from which objectives and targets can be drawn. From that point, we can monitor and measure progress over time. In some cases, progress might be phenomenal, in others level of progress might cause concern, but the availability of an initial assessment is essential to begin that monitoring process. Without these early descriptors, we can underestimate or miss out on all those developments occurring in the child's acquisition of English before they reach the relatively high standards of Level 2. Take another look at Level 2 for English speaking and listening. I would love to be able to achieve all that in Turkish!

The following vignette shows a newly appointed EAL advisory teacher beginning to use the QCA's *A Language in Common* (2000).

S is a 6 year old Bangladeshi girl in this school who arrived three months previously to live with her father at her uncle and aunt's house. I had already set up a home school contact book and tried to involve the aunt (main carer who speaks little English) and her daughter, S's cousin, to help. I had explained the importance of continuing to speak in Bengali with S and the importance of involving S's cousin in home school liaison.

S was currently participating quite well in parts of lessons and seemed happy. She had acquired several words and a few social phrases. She enjoyed drawing and

---

was copy writing proficiently in English (she had not been literate in Bengali). Her teacher and I were concerned however that she could now participate more but often chose to switch off and look at a book.

First, as suggested in Marking Progress (DfES, 2005b) we decided to collect evidence. We recorded S in a guided reading session with her teacher and three other pupils. They were reading a reading scheme book. S was clearly understanding simple what and where questions with visual clues that she could point to and was becoming familiar with the characters in the reading scheme. She was unsure of who questions.

I then had a planning session with S's class teacher. We looked at Language in Common and felt that S had consolidated Step 1 and was now working in Step 2 for both speaking and listening. We wanted to extend her responses into more phrases and to move her toward using process talk, which would be in situation-embedded learning situations as cited by Gibbons (1993) as the first stage of communication

Thus we looked at the medium term literacy and science plans on Growing. S's main Learning Intention would be to understand and use a wider range of action verbs eg it's growing, she's digging. We identified plenty of context embedded situations which would help S to achieve this.

At a whole school staff meeting I introduced *A Language in Common* and gave an example of one of the pupils' assessment profiles. I talked about how we had planned collaboratively from the starting point of the assessment.

Subsequent oral and written assessments showed improvement. S's class teacher showed me that she had included her *Language in Common* assessment in her end of term report. Overall my reflections led me to conclude that EAL learners must be planned for, no matter how few in number they are.

The position relating to EAL and special educational needs (SEN) has been clearly stated on many occasions and is addressed in another chapter of this book. In terms of assessment, the importance of monitoring progress over time cannot be overemphasised.

A child acquires English most effectively from interaction with peers, particularly when peers can provide good models of language for that child. A child also acquires English through the language of the curriculum when this is made accessible by teachers. Time is another important element. These three factors alone can provide the child with everything they need to acquire English and to participate effectively in class through the curriculum. If a child is placed with a group which does not supply these criteria, even if the group does have additional adult support, the results will not be so effective, either for the acquisition of English or for maintaining the self esteem of the child. What might seem a solution to support the child might actually have a detrimental effect. In terms of methods of assessment, descriptors that have been developed for assessing pupils with SEN are not appropriate for EAL.

In the current climate of *Every Child Matters* (DfES, 2004b) and personalised learning, schools are attempting to do their best to meet each individual child's needs and reach out to the community from which they come. Assessment has its place in this broad scenario, as it forms a part of looking beyond the superficialities of the child and recognising that the isolated child does not speak English. It identifies the strengths and abilities of the child, reaches out and involves the family of the child and provides a structure in which progress and ability can be measured, recognised and celebrated.

Judith Howard is a specialist teacher with Hampshire Ethnic Minority Achievement Service. She contributed to the development of 'Marking Progress' and has trained schools extensively in the assessment of bilingual learners, particularly those in isolated contexts.

5

Inclusive strategies for teaching bilingual learners with SEN in mainstream schools

Lisa Kalm and Jenny May

Schools new to working with isolated bilingual learners inevitably face challenges. When isolated bilingual learners have potential learning difficulties then the challenges can appear even greater. The principles involved remain the same however. In fact inclusive approaches need to be enhanced rather than diminished.

It is important to find out the educational and cultural background of such learners as this might provide clues to difficulties especially when there is no help at hand. Furthermore it is important to consider cultural and language support, including for the family, in any placement. Perhaps this consideration even comes above specialist support for a particular learning difficulty. A focus on starting with understanding of meaning and then moving to understanding of isolated words or parts of words is also important, providing as it does a route into interaction for learning.

This chapter tackles the issues of identification of bilingual learners with special educational needs and provision for them.

In order to make appropriate provision for bilingual learners with Special Educational Needs (SEN) it is first essential to be as certain as possible that the learners concerned do in fact have both EAL (English as an Additional Language) and SEN needs. The *SEN Code of Practice* (DfES, 2001) makes a clear distinction between learning difficulties and EAL:

> A child must not be regarded as having a learning difficulty solely because the language or form of language of the home is different from the language in which he or she will be taught.

Despite this guidance, confusion still exists over the identification of bilingual learners with SEN. Although it is much rarer to find schools identifying children as having SEN purely because they speak another language at home than it was before the Code of Practice first came into force, there are still cases where bilingual learners are incorrectly identified as having SEN. Many of these learners are just in the process of acquiring English as an Additional Language and do not have any form of additional learning difficulty. They require EAL teaching strategies and support, but not SEN provision.

Conversely, in other cases, schools can be too cautious about the identification of SEN in bilingual children. This could be due to them not having a clear understanding of how to assess bilingual learners for SEN or because they are worried about incorrectly identifying a child as having SEN when they are just in the early stages of learning English. Sometimes staff incorrectly think that a child only has EAL needs when they in fact also have a learning difficulty. This lack of identification of SEN results in the children concerned not receiving the appropriate provision in the classroom, which can in turn adversely affect their levels of progress and self-esteem.

Currently, research has shown that certain groups of bilingual learners are over or under represented compared to their white monolingual peers in terms of the identification of different types of SEN. Lindsay, Pather and Strand (2006) studied data on 6.5 million pupils by ethnic group and found the following:

Over-representation:
- **Bangladeshi pupils**: hearing impairment (HI)

- **Pakistani pupils**: visual impairment (VI), HI, multi-sensory impairment (MSI) and profound and multiple learning difficulties (PMLD)

- **Chinese pupils**: speech and language and communication needs (SLCN)

Under-representation:

- **Black African pupils**: Moderate Learning Difficulties (MLD), Specific Learning Difficulties (SpLD), Behavioural, Emotional and Social Difficulties (BESD) and Physical Disabilities (PD)

- **Black Other pupils**: MLD, VI and PD

- **Indian, Bangladeshi, Pakistani, Asian Other pupils**: BESD, SpLD and Autistic Spectrum Disorder (ASD)

- **Indian, Bangladeshi, Asian Other pupils**: MLD

- **Chinese**: BESD, SpLD and MLD

Whilst some of the differences, eg over-representation of sensory impairment and physical disabilities, can be put down to genetic factors resulting from the prevalence of consanguinity within certain ethnic groups, others are likely to be the result of misidentification of pupils' needs. For example, the over-representation of Chinese pupils in the SLCN category could be a result of a lack of understanding of early EAL development in Chinese speaking children; difficulties in pronunciation of some words in English could be due to certain sounds not being present in Chinese. However, the under-representation of bilingual pupils with SEN is currently perhaps more of a concern; particularly within the MLD, SpLD, and ASD categories where it is often school staff who are involved in raising an initial cause for concern. If accurate identification is not achieved, bilingual learners with SEN will not be given the most appropriate provision and may not achieve their potential.

Accurate identification of bilingual learners with SEN is not always easy or straightforward. It may take considerable time to assess with certainty, perhaps up to six months. In order to make an assessment of SEN in a bilingual learner, a wide range of background information and evidence about the pupil must be gathered, often from a variety of sources including parents and other professionals. The following section gives guidance on the types of information that need to be considered as well as highlighting other factors that may affect the achievement of pupils with EAL – 'learning difficulties do not always result from problems within the pupil' (Rosamond *et al*, 2003).

Assessment of bilingual pupils with SEN

Newly arrived children who are acquiring English should be assessed according to the extended scales set out in *A Language in Common – assessing English as an Additional Language* (QCA, 2000). The criteria for speaking, listening, reading and writing describe a pupil's development at two steps before Level 1 in the National Curriculum.

The Special Educational Needs and Disability Update (DfES, 2004c) states:

> P scales should not be applied to recently arrived pupils and/or those new to English unless it has been established that a special need (6.14-6.16 of the SEN Code of Practice) is likely to be the only reason for performance below the expected level.

Pupils need to be assessed over a range of subjects and tasks. The pupil's background also needs to be taken into account.

Parental involvement

Before the child enters the school, the parents should be invited to a parental conferencing session, with an interpreter if necessary, so that the following background information can be obtained:

- language/s spoken and understood
- language development ie at what age the child started to speak, and their fluency
- previous educational background, especially the age of starting school, any gaps in education and grades achieved
- any health issues or developmental delays
- religious and cultural issues the school needs to be aware of
- the child's hobbies and interests
- length of stay in the UK
- frequency and length of extended visits to the country of origin
- trauma and racism experienced by the child or the family
- isolation in the community or whether members of the extended family are within easy travelling distance

Teachers may need to have the help of a bilingual assistant to obtain information on:

- fluency in the first language: Are the sentences grammatically correct? Is the vocabulary age appropriate?

- the extent of literacy in the first language

- pupil's understanding of the curriculum

Factors affecting achievement
Teachers need to be aware of:

- pupils new to English who are going through the **silent period**. This can last up to a year and far from being a passive time, the child is actively involved in tuning into English and trying to make sense of it

- any overt **racism** experienced by the child or family at school or in the community

- **attendance** issues

- **cultural issues** regarding children with special needs: it is not uncommon for some children to remain at home rather than enter the education system.

- **different practices in education** in other countries, especially where pupils have to pass an exam in order to go into the next class. Some pupils may have repeated one or two years in the same class and be working with younger pupils

- **curriculum differences** in other countries: a book-based science curriculum may have been studied and letter names rather than letter sounds emphasised

Strategies to use when teaching bilingual learners with SEN
Using a visual approach
Long periods of unsupported talk is meaningless to pupils new to English and will often result in a deterioration of behaviour. Talk supported by visuals will encourage attention and concentration. Pictures, diagrams, artefacts, gestures and demonstrations by peers or adults will aid understanding.

Partnership with parents

■ staff may need to hold frequent meetings with parents, with an interpreter if necessary, so that they are aware of the child's targets and the steps to achieve them

■ some information may need to be translated and parents may require a demonstration of activities to do at home, especially if they did not receive their education in this country

■ information regarding support in the community should be given eg the local group for parents of autistic or deaf children, the national support body for families with dyslexic children etc

■ the use of a home/school liaison book may help parents to reinforce learning in class. If information to parents is written, unknown words can be checked in the dictionary at home. If information is given verbally, some parents may misunderstand and be reluctant to say so

Multi-agency working

Multi-agency work should begin as soon as possible for those who have definite needs with parents being kept informed about those involved and what they can offer eg Educational Psychology Service, Hearing Impaired Service, Behaviour Support Service, Speech and Language Therapist etc.

Use of resources

■ ensure that appropriate visuals and resources eg books and posters show children who share the same culture

■ display word banks and with visuals in the classroom for pupils to use

■ use a visual timetable

■ provide visual response/request cards eg a toilet sign

Use of first language

■ use peers, bilingual assistants and other adults who share the same language to help make the curriculum accessible

- make dual language glossaries of key words with visual clues which can be used by parents as prompts at home to reinforce the curriculum. Some glossaries may need to be supported by oral recordings

- obtain bilingual resources eg books, CDs, books with cassettes or CDs (available from MantraLingua: www.mantralingua.com)

- have a bilingual dictionary, possibly a *talking dictionary* (available from MantraLingua) available in the classroom

- use first language for discussions and planning, eg a story or persuasive writing, especially when cognitive demands are high

Increasing opportunities for talk

All EAL pupils benefit from talking about activities with others and should have the opportunity to be grouped with good peer language models. This will repeat, revise and reinforce new vocabulary and concepts. Talk will help pupils to work out their responses to tasks and pupils with special needs may require more opportunities to talk with visual clues available to make it more meaningful.

Differentiate methods of recording:

- annotate pictures and diagrams

- sequence pictures

- draw diagrams and pictures

- ask an adult to scribe first language and/or English responses

- use the computer and the spellchecker to write up tasks

- use cassette recorders, dictaphones, digital or video cameras to complete tasks

Two case studies will now be described to show how accurate identification and assessment is crucial in putting appropriate strategies into place for bilingual learners with SEN, and how this can lead to very good outcomes for the children concerned.

Case Study 1

Context

A junior school contacted Hampshire Ethnic Minority Achievement (EMA) Service because they were concerned about the lack of progress made by a pupil, Stephen. He was in Year 4 and could copy quickly and neatly, but could not read or write independently, except for his first name. He spoke English fluently and participated well orally in class. His behaviour had recently started to deteriorate.

Background information collected

Stephen came to the United Kingdom from South Africa when he was six years old. He was of mixed race, White and Black African, and Afrikaans was his first language. He started school in the United Kingdom part of the way through Year 1, having had no previous school experience in South Africa due to a later school starting age in his home country.

He settled into school well, received EAL support and picked up spoken English quite quickly. Initially, there were no concerns regarding SEN as it was understood that he would require time to acquire English as an Additional Language and his speaking and listening skills were progressing well.

Whilst in infant school, Stephen developed a range of coping strategies which may have masked the extent of his difficulties from his teacher. He was very adept at using picture clues when reading aloud and could memorise text in reading books quite accurately. He also became a very good copier – he had neat handwriting, and made good use of his peers during writing tasks.

It was not until the beginning of Year 4 that staff began to become concerned over Stephen's lack of progress. His behaviour also began to become a concern – he started to mess about during lessons and did not concentrate well.

Assessment

A Specialist Teacher from Hampshire Ethnic Minority Achievement Service observed Stephen in class. It became clear that he had no difficulty in understanding the concepts taught in class as long as reading was not required. Orally he was quite sharp. During writing tasks he either relied on his peers and copied or attempted to avoid the task by being very slow to get his pencil, finding excuses to leave his seat, or by just copying the date from the board very slowly so that he ran out of time.

Stephen was assessed using the QCA steps from *A Language in Common* (QCA, 2000). It was clear that his reading and writing skills were Step 1, but that his speaking and listening skills were Level 3. He was only able to write his first name and the word 'I' independently. He could not read any other words, although his understanding of stories was generally good due to his use of pictures. It also became clear that he did not have any idea of the relationship between sounds and letters in English. He had no phonic knowledge and a poor visual memory. Although he could copy well, he could not write single letters independently without a visual clue as he could not remember what they looked like.

Stephen was asked what he felt about his own learning in school and admitted to feeling frustrated and embarrassed about his inability to read and write.

Stephen was identified as having Specific Learning Difficulties (SpLD) due to the fact that his learning difficulties related only to the specific areas of reading and writing, and that his overall cognitive ability was probably within the average range.

Strategies
- a teaching assistant (TA) was assigned to work with Stephen for 30 minutes daily. She also supported him in class at other times

- a specialist EMA teacher worked individually with Stephen once a fortnight

- the specialist teacher and TA worked closely with each other. The specialist teacher continually assessed Stephen's progress, fed back to the TA and advised her on what to do next in her daily sessions with him

- specific targets were set and reviewed regularly

- a multisensory programme was used to introduce Stephen to the relationship between letters and sounds; this was practised daily, with lots of repetition and over learning. This was always presented within a meaningful context, usually centred around Stephen's own interests – phonics teaching in isolation does not work well for bilingual learners

■ Stephen was given appropriate reading books – he had previously been attempting books that were far too difficult. He started to follow a structured reading programme aimed at older readers with SEN. Activities around the books were also carried out with the TA, reinforcing and practising new words

■ once Stephen had grasped the relationship between sounds and letters he was encouraged to use his knowledge of initial sounds to write independently for the first time

■ the school with Stephen's mother and explained how she could help him at home

■ Stephen's progress was made clear to him – he could see that he was improving which helped with his self-esteem and behaviour.

■ Stephen was given lots of praise and encouragement.

Outcomes

Stephen made very good progress between Year 4 and Year 5. His reading and writing both increased from Step 1 to Level 1 Secure. His self-esteem rose considerably and his behaviour was no longer a concern. Although his levels of attainment in reading and writing were still low for his year group he was making progress and finding it much easier to take part in classroom activities. If Stephen's SpLD had not been identified and appropriate provision made, he could have reached the end of his primary school education still unable to read and write. With sustained support, Stephen should continue to make good progress.

Case Study 2

Context

Markus was born in the United Kingdom. He was referred to Hampshire Ethnic Minority Achievement (EMA) Service on entry to pre-school as he was a bilingual learner. Staff soon began to suspect that he had SEN in addition to EAL.

Background information collected

As an infant he was slow to talk in his first language (Greek). His parents had begun to use English at home; unfortunately their English had not developed beyond basic level, eg his mother could only use incomplete sentences and a narrow vocabulary. His sister, who was two years older, was the only competent speaker of English in the home. Her Greek was well developed because her early years were spent constantly with the extended family, where Greek was the only language used. Markus did not have the same exposure to Greek, as the family moved away from their extended family when he was a baby.

Assessment

On entry to pre-school, a referral was made to Hampshire EMA Service. The Greek speaking bilingual assistant (BA) reported that Markus' first language skills were extremely limited and that often she could not understand what he was saying. He was unable to respond to simple general questions or instructions. As a result of her report a speech and language therapist was asked to become involved.

Strategies

- his language acquisition started to be closely monitored by the speech and language therapist, pre-school staff and the bilingual assistant

- a language programme was developed for the pre-school staff to follow

- the parents were asked to use Greek at home so that Markus would hear a good model of the language

- the BA provided regular weekly support

- the BA was asked to interpret at a parental conference with the speech and language therapist

- later, parents were advised to apply for a place at an infant school with a language unit

- reports from the speech and language team and the EMA team were provided to support his application

Outcomes

Markus is now in Year 1 and his English is developing well. The staff are fully aware of his needs and his language programme. He works in the mainstream class and also has regular sessions in the language unit. He can count up to 50 and will readily initiate talk. He responds to questions, uses sentences and is able to follow single instructions.

At the end of his reception year the family visited Greece and his parents reported that his understanding and usage of his first language had improved by the end of the visit. Since then, his parents have been using more of their first language at home.

His parents attend the regular review meetings with a bilingual assistant from the EMA service to interpret and support their son's learning and language acquisition at home. He will continue his education at the school for another year and transfer to a junior school with a language unit.

Case Study 3

Context

Sophia was born in Britain into a Gujarati speaking environment and was fairly quickly diagnosed as having a hearing impairment.

Background

The family already had an older daughter with the same condition but the middle daughter and the three sons were unaffected: their hearing was normal. The elder daughter was born in India and had no opportunity to attend school but had stayed at home, helping in the house and with the upbringing of her younger siblings.

Assessment

Regular checks were made by health professionals and, because many of her siblings had received most of their education in Britain, they were able to contribute to the assessment procedure and report back to their parents.

Strategies

- the family members were taught British Sign Language (BSL) so that Sophia would be used to it before she entered school

- the family also continued to use their own sign language which they had developed when their eldest daughter was born. This was necessary so that Sophia could communicate with her sister

- Sophia's primary education was in a school with a hearing impairment unit attached. Her secondary education was in a school for moderate learning difficulties. In both schools signing was used and Sophia was able to communicate effectively

- members of the family who were confident users of English were always available to communicate with professionals

Outcomes

Sophia is able to communicate well with all her family using two different methods of signing. She can also communicate with users of BSL. In her secondary education she developed an aptitude for horticulture and won several prizes.

Since leaving school she has been able to continue her education at a local college. Hopefully, Sophia will be able to follow her middle sister into employment in her chosen field.

Sophia was able to receive an appropriate education because her condition had been diagnosed extremely early and there was suitable provision for her locally. Her eldest sister was unable to attend school and receive an education in India because there was no local provision. Consequently she has not been able to seek employment outside the home environment especially as she cannot use BSL.

Conclusion

In order to put in place suitable support strategies for bilingual pupils, comprehensive assessment needs to be compiled over a period of time. This assessment must take account of the first language and home culture.

Any support put in place needs to be talked through with the parents, using an interpreter if necessary. Parents and school working together can greatly improve the educational experience and overall attainment of the bilingual learner who has special educational needs.

Optimus education, ElectricWord plc have kindly given their written permission for the article 'Inclusive Strategies for Teaching Bilingual Learners with SEN in Mainstream Schools' to be included in this chapter.

Lisa Kalim and Jenny May have worked for Hampshire Ethnic Minority Achievement Service since 2002 and 1992 respectively. Both are specialist teachers with particular expertise in working with pupils who have EAL and SEN. Lisa Kalim mainly works with pupils in Key Stages 2-4, Jenny May within the Foundation Stage and Key Stage 1. Both are involved in advising teachers and other school staff across Hampshire on inclusive strategies for bilingual learners with Special Educational Needs.

6

Working in partnership with parents

Kamaljit Dulai

The Children Act 1989 established the principle that the welfare of the child is the paramount consideration and stressed the importance of developing a partnership with parents. The Children Act 2004/*Every Child Matters* (DfES, 2004b) agenda sets five clear outcomes for children. It is recognised that parents are at the heart of achieving the five outcomes for children. If the parents can improve how they relate to their children, this will be the single most effective way of improving outcomes for children. Research also shows that children learn more from parents than anyone else. Parents are acknowledged as having unique knowledge and information about their children's needs.

> Parental involvement in their child's literacy practices is seen as a more powerful force than other family background variables such as social class, family size and level of parental education. (Flouri and Buchanan, 2004)

Therefore schools need to work in partnership with parents of isolated bilingual learners. A growing number of schools are trying harder to develop more appropriate strategies to enable parents' active participation in their children's education. Developing a home school relationship is not always easy as many parents need extra help. For example, there is often poor representation of parents of isolated bilingual pupils on the school governing bodies and generally in schools. It is widely believed that ethnic minority parents are reluctant or not interested in getting involved in their children's education, which is not true. There is no research evidence to support this view. Schools should try to understand the personal and social reasons why some parents are less able to be involved. At a parents' meeting organised by Hampshire EMA Service, one mother, a secondary school teacher, was asked to comment on her experience of coming to Britain. She told us:

> Although I could speak English, I didn't have the courage to speak to other parents or neighbours and make friends. I lost my self esteem, felt alienated and disempowered and preferred to stay at home most of the time. I even hated going to my children's school events.

Apart from the language barrier there are many other reasons why ethnic minority parents find it really difficult to keep in constant touch with their children's schools. Some of the factors are: lack of time, lack of confidence, lack of information or sometimes too much information from schools, previous experience of racism, feelings of alienation and lack of communication.

The language barrier often affects their self confidence. Parents can feel marginalised from everyday school life and this makes the task of bringing up their children more difficult for them. In some schools, English as an Additional Language is seen as a problem and parents may be treated accordingly.

The experience of racism and discrimination at parents' workplaces creates strains and deters ethnic minority parents from coming forward. They feel that they have nothing to offer or they are not wanted in the school. Many parents feel that the racism they and their children have to face is generally ignored. So they don't trust the authorities. Some parents may hold negative views about teachers because of their past experiences which lead them to feel incapable of taking part in their children's education. As Blatchford (1994) suggests:

> Years of undermined self-confidence and inner articulation of themselves as being incapable could make some parents doubtful about their own ability to be good educators to their own children.

She mentions again: 'until parents can trust the educators there is little point in expecting their active support'.

For some families economic survival is their day to day priority. Some of them work long hours or night shifts so the timing of school events might not be appropriate.

The British education system is different to that of many countries. Some parents may have no idea how to help their children. In some cultures or countries the parents are not supposed to interfere with the teacher's job. Therefore the parents may not be aware of schools' expectations in Britain and may think that educating their children is solely the school's responsibility.

Blatchford also states:

> Parents have different culturally conceived ideas about the role of education and educators. In some cultures the role of the educators is seen as distinct and separate to the role of parenting, and educators many need to take some time explaining and illustrating how the child can benefit from partnership.

Parents who believe they can make a difference in their children's education are more likely to visit and participate in school activities than those who feel ineffective. In discussions with parents:

> it is sensible for educators not to make assumptions about parents' knowledge, beliefs or experiences but to create a friendly atmosphere where parents can talk openly about their feelings. (Blatchford, 1994)

She also suggests that:

> it is almost impossible to represent every parent's views but that is no reason not to find ways of communicating with the full range of parents to get a better balance of perceived parental needs across class, gender, race and disability within the community.

Materials for Schools (DfES, 2003) also stresses that:

> parents need to see changes happening as a result of their contribution. They will then feel part of the process.

What schools can do

Schools need to tackle stereotypes about parents and take responsibility for building confidence by discovering suitable strategies to meet the needs of ethnic minority communities. To encourage parental involvement there are a number of areas to be considered.

First of all there is a need to consider careful strategies for raising the awareness of opportunities to increase parental participation by regular and effective communication. The parents must feel supported and valued before they are expected to work in partnership with schools. In some cases this means that the school might need to support parents and children for several years, using different strategies to win their trust. There must be real and obvious commitment from staff.

Some authorities or schools spend considerable amounts on producing translated materials but many times and for many reasons it doesn't reach the people who really need it. In a few schools, translated information is kept in the school office but not sent out to parents, whereas others send it in the wrong language by making assumptions about parents' spoken language. This can make the parents feel undermined and undervalued. It requires a great deal of effort on the part of local authorities, not only in terms of availability but also how to reach the people in need.

When inviting parents, letters can be used but a personal approach is more effective. Where initial contacts do not work, a home visit by an appropriate member of staff should be considered. The staff need to decide whether an interpreter is required. They need to be flexible about times for meetings and other events and if possible provide crèches, if needed.

Initial contacts need to be friendly and supporting and the atmosphere relaxed and welcoming as the parents may be feeling uneasy. A language rich environment based on children's cultural backgrounds helps to make the parents feel valued. This can be created by displaying multilingual signs, and pictures displayed in the reception and around the classrooms.

The questions to parents should be clear and culturally appropriate. For example a Muslim parent may feel offended if asked what their 'Christian' name is.

A variety of festivals, family life and art and craft materials should be incorporated in the curriculum. Such initiatives provide a good opportunity for teachers and parents to meet each other in a social setting. Kenner believes that cultural materials and activities can act as ice-breakers for communication.

> The staff can start collecting information and artefacts to show real interest in other cultures before asking parents to talk about their culture as well as show interest in bilingual literacy activities at home. (Kenner, 2000).

But the parents' role should be more than merely as cultural encyclopaedias. They should be involved in the curriculum for example by: giving talks, contributing to story telling or history or geography projects. Schools should take measures to ensure that ethnic minority parents are as proportionately involved as other parents on the governing bodies, assistance in class and fundraising.

Teachers must develop an understanding of children's cultural backgrounds in order to integrate children's cultural experiences into their lessons. This can be done by using multicultural resources which reflect children's lives, for example, posters, utensils, puzzles, games and music tapes. As well as informing oneself of relevant research, up-dating staff training and having appropriate resources and learning materials, it is vital for the staff to liaise with parents. Such liaison not only benefits staff and children but also provides an opportunity to give a voice to parents.

Improving parental participation

In 2000, several schools, concerned about the low number of parents from minority groups participating in school life, approached Hampshire EMA Service for advice and support. A survey was conducted in ten schools where there were larger numbers of ethnic minority population. It revealed that many ethnic minority families, scattered throughout Hampshire, felt isolated and cut off from the support of their communities and so had difficulty maintaining their cultural and linguistic heritage. Few of the parents surveyed had had any first hand experience of the British education system and many felt unsure of how best to help their children.

Hampshire EMA Service applied for funding and in 2001 was awarded grants from New Opportunity Funding and Single Regeneration Budget to set up after school clubs. As a result, three homework clubs and three heritage language classes were started in targeted schools and community centres.

Since then Hampshire EMA Service has played a vital role to help improve parental participation by working together with schools and parents to run different projects in many schools, for example homework clubs, heritage language classes, family learning and access to learning projects in which parents learn about education in the UK and can learn about educational opportunities for themselves. As *Materials for Schools* says:

Working effectively with parents is assumed to be something that teachers will auto-matically learn and take on, without training or support. (DfES, 2003)

However, many schools have now given responsibility to senior members of staff to develop strategies for closer involvement with parents and some have even appointed home school liaison officers, many of them bi-lingual, to have direct contact with ethnic minority families.

It has not as yet been possible to monitor fully the impact of these initia-tives on increase in parental involvement in schools but some outcomes from the Hampshire Access to Learning Project noted are:

- A father, highly educated in Nepal, very keen to find out about local government jobs, signposted to social services, police and council offices

- A mother, anxious to find ways to support her children with their school work, arranged a meeting with her children's teachers

- Husband will not allow his wife to study outside the home with other people, possible issue of domestic violence

- One Chinese speaking family recently attended a family laptop learning evening after being told about it at the school's ESOL course

- A mother who participated in a school workshop showed a talent for telling rhymes in her first language and was invited to help with an after school language club at a local junior school. She has now enrolled on a childcare course at the local college

- One father has asked for training in word processing which could help him with his business as well as his status in the eyes of his young children

There may still only be a small number of ethnic minority governors in Hampshire but the number increased from 40 for 540 schools in 2001 to 94 for 540 schools in 2006. Parental involvement has been a key aspect of a school chosen to illustrate good practice for the national *New Arrivals Excellence Programme* in 2007 (DfES and DCSF) and the following des-cription accurately shows an increasing picture in Hampshire schools:

The school has a vibrant and welcoming reception area with toys for toddlers. There are rich displays all round the school celebrating the richness and diversity of its parents and children. The receptionist has a very good rapport with staff, parents and children. According to Mrs S, a Hindi speaking parent, 'Initially I was so worried and confused regarding the admission of my daughter. My friend told me to talk to Mrs J. She is so polite and approachable, if I have any concerns I always come and talk to her'.

There are seven Hindi speaking children in the reception class. Their parents are on short term contracts with accommodation provided near the school. The parents have very high expectations of their children. They have experience of a very formal style of teaching and learning so have lots of questions about their children's school and education. For example, the children are not getting enough homework and they are playing most of the time.

The class teacher arranged for the Hindi speaking bilingual assistant to meet the parents and answer their questions. The parents were invited to a topic sharing morning for the topics on autumn and the picture book *Elmer* (McKee, 1989) which illustrates the value of being different. All the Hindi speaking mothers came for the morning, walked round the school building, collected leaves with their children and sat with them for the story time. It was an excellent opportunity for them to feel valued, find out about the class topic, how the children are taught and how they can help at home.

Of course it helped that there were seven children speaking the same language, but all these features of an inclusive school could be in place for one or two children.

Kamaljit Dulai has worked for Hampshire Ethnic Minority Achievement Service as a bilingual assistant since 1994 and for the past seven years she has been managing a team of bilingual assistants. As part of her role she has worked on various projects to encourage representation of parents of ethnic minority pupils on school governing bodies and generally in schools.

7

Valuing people: reaching isolated ethnic minority people with learning disabilities and their families

Dominique Rawlings

I n 2001, the government White Paper, *Valuing People: a new strategy for learning disability for the 21st century* (Department of Health, 2001) set the agenda for change for learning disability services; in particular, it acknowledged that the needs of people from ethnic minority communities were often overlooked and that many parents, especially those from minority communities, needed more support to care for their children. It also recommended that better information be made available to them. Previous chapters have dealt with the identification and inclusion of bilingual learners with Special Educational Needs (SEN) and with the importance of involving parents and families in school life. Challenges in reaching and engaging families have been highlighted and examples of successful practice presented. This chapter, while building on previous ones, moves away from a strictly school context to consider not only the pupil but rather the child, young person or adult with learning disabilities and describes the issues they and their families face when they live in areas of relatively small ethnic minority visible presence. It also discusses how services may successfully engage with them. Schools, but also other professionals, will be interested in the issues highlighted and practice example offered. By raising their awareness, they will be better equipped to work co-operatively in multi agency situations to ensure that 'every disabled isolated ethnic minority child matters'.

Hampshire is a large and predominantly rural county with relatively small and widely dispersed ethnic minority communities (CVS consultants, 2004). Figures from the 2001 census suggest that the ethnic minority presence in Hampshire, while still below the national average, had increased by 73 per cent since the previous census. More recent data from local services and the voluntary sector suggest a further, accelerating growth. This is partly but by no means solely due to the arrival of white minority groups from Eastern Europe. Indeed, diversity of origins has also increased; for example, the Hampshire EMA service now receives referrals for over 100 different languages. Ethnic minority settlement has remained dispersed although some particular patterns of concentration are emerging in two areas in the north of the county. As this is very recent, communities are seldom organised or represented, making it difficult for service providers to identify them and engage with them.

This chapter uses the term ethnic minority to refer to all those who categorise themselves as an ethnic group other than White British which also includes Travellers. The term learning disabilities is used widely although it is acknowledged that some people prefer the term learning difficulties. Experience and practice presented are based on the Social Model of disability, which recognizes that everyone is equal and that it is society that erects barriers preventing and restricting disabled people's participation. In this chapter, it is strongly acknowledged that people with learning disabilities and/or difficulties are people first, with their own culture, language, community and aspirations.

Available research and literature on the low take up of learning disability services by members of minority groups identify a number of barriers that this population faces; these include communication (Office for Public Management, 2006), lack of information and monitoring systems, lack of policy impact assessment (Hatton nd cited by Office for Public Management, 2006), a western approach to modern learning disability concepts, such as independence and inclusion, which may be at odds with some cultures (Bignall and Butt, 2000) and a lack of culturally appropriate provision (Valuing People Support Team, nd). These issues were identified through research mainly in large established communities. Experience of the ethnic minority learning disability (EMLD) project over the last two years shows that they apply even more for people who live outside big urban centres, in areas with little ethnic minority presence. Indeed isolation can make an issue become an insurmountable barrier.

Communication

When there is no identified population pocket and a wide range of languages spoken, it is difficult to provide generic translated material that will answer the needs of all. Translation has to be done on a requested basis and this can take time, initially creating frustration and later resignation and disengagement. It is also more difficult to find an interpreter as few ethnic minority support workers will be in place. An over reliance on generic translated material has also been found to be ineffective because of people's different level of literacy in their home language, and because of the inadequate translation of some technical terms that simply don't translate in some languages or only in a very high register. Many times, a project worker would talk to families prepared with translated material only to be asked if the English version could be provided instead: parents or carers wanted to ask a younger family member to explain the information at home; this young person would often have been educated in Britain and therefore would speak the home language but only be literate in English. So it emerged that better communication could be achieved by oral explanations in the home language, backed up with English language written ones. This had the added advantage of providing the opportunity to teach the family a number of key words in English that made them better equipped when dealing with other services and thus empowered them.

Betancourt, Green and Carillo (2002) had found that access to a professional who could give verbal advice in the home language was the best way of communicating and overcoming the home language literacy issue. Mir and Din (2003) also advocated that access to this person should be easy; it should not rely on professional referral and should be advertised widely through outreach activities and through networks used by ethnic minority communities.

A large part of the EMLD project work consists in outreach activities and in going to meet groups and community or faith leaders. Personal contacts are established and fostered; the support available through the project is explained and advertised.

Because it is situated within the EMA service, the project is able to use bilingual assistants to help with communication; this means that information in the home language can be provided relatively easily and promptly. Experience has also shown that perseverance is essential to foster successful contact with families and individuals. Having a language resource that can be used promptly and easily for regular liaison, to remind people of appointments or to repeat explanations to a different family member can make all the difference. Services can then engage with individuals and families much more efficiently.

Peter is five and has recently started school. School staff soon developed concerns about his behaviour. They were also concerned that communication with parents, although apparently successfully understood as one parent spoke English, did not often lead to the requested action. It was assumed that the parents did not want to engage with school and other professionals. A meeting of professionals, school staff and specialist bilingual staff who had worked with Peter in Early Years concluded that a statutory assessment process should be initiated. The EMLD project supported the parents by explaining the reasons for this recommendation and by explaining the different options and choices.

A bilingual assistant was involved. This meant that both parents were able to understand all the information provided. Her involvement was not limited to one meeting and that is what made the difference. She would call the parents time and time again to remind them of the different forms to fill in, to explain the need to keep appointments with other professionals or to explain about transport. Her regular and immediate response to relay small but significant information from professionals meant that Peter, who since early childhood had slipped through the net and not received any appropriate support, could finally start making progress.

Culture
Newly arrived people may not have any relatives or respected community figures to turn to for advice. There may be no support groups or even families in similar situations who could empathise with them and offer advice. In some cultures, this is exacerbated as there is still a stigma

attached to learning disabilities together with strong competitiveness amongst families and the need to appear successful. Some families may feel they want to keep a member with learning disabilities hidden. Virgo (2006) in a research commissioned by Mencap had found that carers from black and minority ethnic communities were often left to cope alone as they did not receive help from their own community; one carer had told her:

> I don't know anyone else who has a child with this condition. I feel that I am not doing enough for her and I don't know where to turn for help.

It was also found that, generally, people would not turn down support offered but too often they did not know it could be provided, or where to ask for it.

Many families who are unfamiliar with welfare and social services, because of lack of similar services in their home country, regard workers from these services with suspicion. There is often still a worry that their family member might be taken away. Conversely, people coming from countries where disabled people are segregated do not always understand and may feel abandoned by services which offer only mainstream options. They may feel that their family member would be better cared for in segregated, specialist settings. Inclusion is not a concept that is readily understood by people who come from societies where this is not developed. There is a strong need to explain how learning disabilities services have evolved in Britain over the last twenty years; this will help families to understand why specific inclusive options are offered and reassure them that they are benefiting from the best practice in this country.

In areas where there is no identified concentration of particular communities, the argument for dedicated, specialist provision is difficult to sustain. However, support services should make themselves more aware of what may constitute barriers for some ethnic minority individuals so that they can remain open to adapting their practice to the needs of individuals. They do not need to develop an extensive specialist knowledge of the many cultures that are present in the county. Indeed, even if they have such knowledge, they need to remain alert to the fact that every individual and family is different and that culture is a largely personal experience. They need to develop the empathy and understanding of what aspect of their practice may constitute a barrier and be creative and reflexive enough to change it.

Cultural competence training can help a lot with this. It should be available to every member of a service and particularly front line and reception workers as it is a successful first engagement that can make all the difference. Husain (2005) explains that it should never be assumed that a client's ethnicity or colour says anything about their cultural values, religious beliefs or behaviour and that cultural knowledge based on assumptions and stereotypes is ignorance. Instead, she advocates a model of cultural competence practice based on knowledge, awareness and sensitivity, supported by effective communication.

Community engagement and training

Mir and Tovey (2002) found that engaging with community groups can help to transfer the cultural competence located in these groups to service providers. They also suggested that such groups would need to be developed in areas where they do not already exist. In Hampshire, because the ethnic minority presence is still developing while remaining geographically dispersed, there are very few groups to engage with. This is why an EMLD project worker is also assisting the local population, in one particular town, to form a diversity forum. This allows her to raise the profile of the project in that area so that it is recognised as a trustworthy partner as well as empowering local people to become valued interlocutors for the project's future consultations.

There is a great need for information, as described above, not only for individuals and families on specific issues, but also to raise awareness generally within newly arrived populations of the availability of support services and of the principles that underpin them. One carer had told Virgo (2006):

> When you ask me what I need to help, I don't know what to say. I don't know enough about learning disability to know what it is I need to know.

Through awareness raising exercises and public debate, it becomes much more socially acceptable to talk about learning disability issues and individuals in need of support are less likely to remain hidden as their families develop the confidence and basic knowledge to approach services.

Right from the start, the EMLD project found that people rarely understood the words learning disability. It was also found that the best way to provide an explanation was to use a visual support, not only as it attracted people's attention better than mere words and scientific definitions, but also because it showed real people and the positive, rather than the restrictive aspects of their life. A film was developed for this purpose: it shows ethnic minority people with learning disabilities achieving (for example going to college) and making choices in their life. It features advocates supporting them with these choices and this helps to explain the role of advocacy, which is also often poorly understood. It proved to be a great resource to raise interest, start debate and increase knowledge.

Dispersed populations may appear hard to reach. Using community and ethnic radio stations can help. Several radio programmes were broadcast on learning disability issues and to publicise the EMLD project. They generated calls from listeners and raised public awareness. Two of these programmes were broadcast in both English and a community language. They helped raise the awareness and understanding of listeners but also of the interpreters who, as well respected figures in their community, have also become much more knowledgeable about advising, empathising with and signposting newly arrived families with disabled members.

The following extract from an article on the developments (Wardak, 2007) describes the rationale for the broadcasts.

In many cases, the community leaders were not able to help their community members, as they are not in touch with different services available in the city.

In order to respond to the networking needs of the communities a monthly radio programme has been arranged for both communities [Somali and Afghan].

The Afghan community has a Community Hour Radio Programme every last Wednesday of the month broadcasted by the Community Radio Unity 101. The Chairperson of Afghan Community hosts the radio programme. Service Managers from different agencies are invited and the programme takes place in three languages, Pashto, Dari and English. The Afghan Community also takes part in the programme and gets the answers of their queries directly.

It creates a kind of professional relationship between the service managers, the voluntary sector and the community leaders. Through the radio programme, the

---

community leaders were engaged in raising awareness of learning disability and other services among their respective communities. The radio programme also gives the opportunity to the service providers to engage community leaders in improving their existing services. Leaders sometimes subsequently attend further service events.

It helps the community leaders to understand the different aspects of the existing services and changes in the future. Community Leaders also mentioned that participation in such events help integrate with English community and increases communication channels.

Innovative projects can also help raise awareness in a positive, non threatening way. This was the case of the Community Tree Project, which ran, in 2006, in partnership with the Hampshire Museum Service.

This project helped to publicise the work of the Ethnic Minority Learning Disability project in the community. The meetings were informal and both interviewers and interviewees had a positive role. It created the opportunity for ethnic minority people to meet people with learning disabilities and this helped them understand present day learning disability services concepts such as independence, inclusion, support workers and advocacy. As they met and interviewed individuals rather than organisations, they overcame the fact that there were few organisations to approach in their area.

Recording and monitoring

A lack of consistent data on the ethnic make up of the population and on the take up of services can prevent their correct targeting; issues are less likely to be identified as they arise. Increasingly, joint working of social care and NHS teams highlighted the need to develop a consistent approach to ethnicity recording. Equally, in children's services, although practice has improved to record ethnicity of pupils generally, this is still not achieved consistently for pupils with a Statement of Special Educational Needs. This could be due to the fact that the recording of ethnicity relies on the school of destination; these may include a variety of settings, some independent, some outside the county.

It has also been found that many professionals and settings have a tendency to concentrate on addressing the disability needs rather than con-

The story behind the Community Tree

From idea to exhibition

- The Museum Service wanted to create an exhibition to show that there are people from many different cultures who live in Hampshire. They asked the Ethnic Minority Learning Disability Project for help with ideas.

- Together, they thought it would be a good idea to collect stories from people. They thought they would ask them to talk about an object or a picture as this would make the exhibition more interesting for the visitors.

- They thought they would call it "Community Tree" because a tree has many leaves, like a book, and each leaf can be a different story. All the leaves grow together on the same tree like all the people live here.

- Hampshire Partnership Board also thought this was a good idea and gave some funding.

- People from advocacy projects said they would like to be part of this project. They agreed to go and interview people from different cultures and find out their stories. They were the *Interviewers*.

- The Ethnic Minority Learning Disability Project worked with Community Development Officers to organise some meetings between the interviewers and the persons who had agreed to be interviewed and tell their stories.

- The interviewers and their support workers worked really hard to prepare their questions. They bought and learnt to use different equipment to be able to record people's stories. Then, finally, they went to the meetings, listened, asked questions, took pictures, learnt lots and...

▪ *Had a great time!*

- They gave the information they had collected, all the objects, the films, picture and recordings to the display team of the museum.

- One week before the launch, everybody met at the museum to help set up the exhibition.

We are very pleased that you chose to come and visit this exhibition. We hope that, like us, you will find it very interesting and think...

It is absolutely brilliant!

Figure 7.1: Extract from the Community Tree display

sidering all needs, language, culture and special needs, equally, from the start. Ethnic recording has great value at a strategic level for addressing developing issues, for planning and for monitoring diversity and equality. It can also be of equally great importance at an operational level. Indeed, enquiring about ethnicity and explaining to a client why this must be recorded, creates an opportunity to find out about their and their family's culture, right at the initial contact. A fruitful dialogue can be initiated on how best to meet all needs.

In some training sessions organised by the EMLD project, it was often found that professionals as well as reception staff felt ill at ease about approaching the subject of cultural needs; they felt embarrassed to ask questions which, from their perspective, seemed intrusive. Training helped many to overcome this, especially as it involved asking questions directly to members of different communities who were invited to take part in the sessions. Many were surprised to see that their questions, far from causing offence, were welcomed as they showed they had a genuine interest in their client. It also allowed participants to practice asking questions sensitively and many reported a great increase in confidence when enquiring about cultural needs. Husain (2005) had also found that people generally welcomed the opportunity to talk about their culture.

Dealing with professionals and agencies

As children grow and prepare to engage in adult life, the number of choices to be made increases. For many newly arrived families and individuals, this can be a very worrying time. If the child has been in the country for a few years, attended school and been assessed in Britain, the chance is that parents will have developed a basic knowledge and understanding of the need to have involvement with different professionals, even though, up to then, this will have mainly included health and education. If at school, a child might have had the opportunity to develop a transition portfolio which will have initiated contact with social care workers and Connexions advisers. They might also have become more aware of training or further education opportunities. Not all children have this chance especially if they arrive in Britain at fifteen or sixteen or even older. While up to age fourteen support and interventions are neatly organised around education and the school, it all changes when the child grows older. Parents may feel lost with the new agencies they need to contact; they may not realise who they need to contact. Very often, it was found, parents were unaware of why specific assessments were made and by whom; they were unable to understand how specific persons were key for specific issues. Many reported that they would like just one person to deal with. This demonstrated the importance of offering a single point of contact, like the EMLD project co-ordinator who can alert and signpost, liaise as well as support parents and individuals in contacting the right agencies.

Raj is sixteen. He came in Britain when he was fifteen. He has moderate physical and learning disabilities. When they first arrived in Britain, Raj's parents were offered the choice of mainstream or special school. They understood what it meant but were not sure how to choose. In the end, they chose the special school as they thought the social worker they had met and who had assessed Raj recommended it. Raj felt very frustrated at school because he found it too easy compared to what he had learnt in his previous school. At the end of the year, he was offered a place at college, on a Skills for Life course. He did not know that there were other courses he might be able to attend; he didn't know who to ask, he was again frustrated with the course's content.

During the summer, Raj's parents were trying to contact the social worker who had initially assessed Raj but with no success. In fact, the worker had closed Raj's case but his parents had not understood that. They also did not understand that that worker was based in the Children with Disability Team in another town; they could not find anyone in their local town social care team to answer their queries as Raj's case was being passed from Children to Transition (for children from age fourteen going through transition from school to other setting) social care teams. They felt lost and did not know who to ask for information. The EMLD project co-ordinator became involved and made contact with the different care teams; appointments were also made with a Connexions adviser and with an advocate who worked with Raj so that his voice and choices could be heard.

Conclusion
Isolated ethnic minority individuals and families with learning disabilities face many barriers to access the support they need. Communication, language, lack of understanding and awareness of the availability of support

services are the greatest of these barriers. But they are not insurmountable. Isolated populations can be reached, using different media and innovative projects. Low numbers might mean that it is not practical to set up specialist provision but with training, sensitivity and responsiveness, existing services can be adapted to meet the need of their ethnic minority clients. A person who is a single point of access and information, and who has developed multi agency working links, both with children and adult services, can be of great value to isolated families and support them to access and receive the support they need and are entitled to. Such a person can contribute to the possibility of a client leading a happy and fulfilling life.

Dominique Rawlings has been part of Hampshire Ethnic Minority Achievement Service for the last eight years. Involved in different projects, she has, in the last two years, been developing the Hampshire Ethnic Minority Learning Disability Project (EMLD) for the county Learning Disability Partnership Board. EMLD is funded by the Hampshire Learning Disability Partnership Board and works in partnership with two advocacy groups: Speakeasy in Basingstoke and the Eastleigh Advocacy Project. The aim of the project is to be a two way link between individuals, adults or children and their families and service providers. It provides signposting and support to ethnic minority people on learning disability issues; it also offers cultural competence training and help with communication issues to service providers.

8

Pupils' experience of racism

Sarah Coles

In this chapter I present two case studies carried out in secondary schools in Hampshire. In each school a questionnaire was used to elicit pupils' experiences and views of racism. The aim was to use the findings from the analysis of the questionnaire data to raise awareness and to provide a focus for targeted intervention.

Having gone through the results from the questionnaire, I discuss the subsequent actions taken by the two schools and consider factors which may have limited the scope of the schools' follow-up activities.

Racism in mainly white British schools

No Problem Here (1987), *Still No Problem Here* (1995), *We're All White, Thanks* (2005) – some twenty years separate these books by Chris Gaine but the issues he raises remain the same and are the arguments for 'consistently addressing race equality in schools where some may still think the small numbers of black and minority ethnic pupils do not warrant the effort' (Gaine, 2005). So what is the link between racism and isolated bilingual learners?

While many teachers sincerely believe that no significant levels of hostility between pupils from different ethnic backgrounds exist, the experiences of isolated pupils from minority ethnic backgrounds in schools in Hampshire in the early part of the 21st century tell a different story. For many of these pupils, an intrinsic part of the school day consists of low level, racist bullying from members of their peer group with much of the hostility occurring outside of the classroom in a world from which teachers are excluded.

Any pupil will be more likely to enjoy and achieve if they feel comfortable and happy at school and are not, along with their PE kit and book bag, lugging excess emotional baggage from lesson to lesson. But the voices of isolated bilingual learners can easily be lost in the mêlée of the school where they make up less than 10 per cent of the population. How do you make yourself heard if you are very new to English? What if nobody else at your school speaks your language? Or understands how very different your previous school was? Your new teachers are generally kind and try to be supportive but you can't convey to them what you are finding difficult or what kind of help you need. And what about the lonely break times with no one to talk to? Or the strange looks some people seem to give you? The odd push in the corridor? The way other students constantly make fun of your accent? Is this normal in a British school?

Often pupils choose to suffer in silence, believing their situation will get worse if they report what is really going on in the corridors between lessons or the playground during break times. Isolated already, they do not wish to give others any more reason to marginalise them. Due to their lack of familiarity with the dominant culture of the school, they may feel that they have neither power nor, if they lack proficiency in English, voice. Some say they just don't think teachers will take them seriously or believe them. Some are scared of reprisals. All are vulnerable and at risk of failing to achieve their potential.

For most of us it is easier simply to avoid talking about the emotive, highly sensitive topic of racism. To identify it is difficult enough: one person's racist incident is another's inconvenient break time squabble, not serious enough to warrant the additional paperwork. Even the necessary voca-bulary is tricky, being subject to frequent change according to the politics of the moment. It may be that some of us are not confident enough to enter such uncomfortable territory, perhaps for fear of making things worse. And it is perhaps not only incidents involving pupils which would need to be addressed but also attitudes voiced in the staff room: we might not want to be the one to open that particular can of worms. Or it may be that, as Gaine suggests, some of us have not examined [our] own assumptions and preconceptions about 'race', immigration and prejudice, so the things pupils say might not grate on [our] ears the way they would on others'. For those who do not consider this issue important, pupils' attitudes are simply part of the background noise; they do not register. (Gaine, 1995)

So, in some schools it can happen that collusion between pupils, teachers and institutional ethos and practice serves to perpetuate a *status quo* wherein a subculture of racism, largely unchallenged and unchecked, persists. For isolated bilingual pupils, it is very clear where, in such circumstances, the power lies.

None of this is new. Over twenty years ago, the Swann Report (DES, 1985) concluded there was

...widespread evidence of racism in all the areas covered, ranging from un-intentional racism and patronising and stereotyped ideas about ethnic minority groups combined with an appalling ignorance of their cultural backgrounds and lifestyles and of the facts of race and immigration, to extremes of overt racial hatred and 'National Front style attitudes... (DES, 1985)

In Hampshire, recent trends in the recording and reporting of racist incidents have shown an increase at all key stages over the last few years, the majority of which are categorised as pupil-to-pupil racist name-calling. (www3.hants.gov.uk/education/hias/intercultural/intercultural-race equality.htm). This is still likely to be the small tip of a very large iceberg as it deals exclusively with reported and recorded incidents; many incidents are not reported at all, some may be reported but not recorded as racist incidents while institutionally racist practices are much more intractable, being harder to identify and tackle successfully. Persistent low-level attacks, verbal and physical, on pupils from minority ethnic backgrounds can easily develop into more serious incidents, sometimes off-site and sometimes involving the use of weapons and attracting the attentions of the police and local – or even national – media.

The riots in Bradford, Oldham and Burnley in 2001 or Birmingham in 2005; the murders of Stephen Lawrence in 1993, Zahid Mubarek in 2000, Kriss Donald in 2004, Anthony Walker in 2005, Mohammad Parvaiz in 2006 or Marlon Moran in May 2007; the shooting of Abu Kamara and Evans Baptiste by a 24 year old British National Party supporter in May 2006; it would seem likely that it is only a matter of time before the next racially-motivated headline story hits the streets. The question is, where do the attitudes that lead people to commit such appalling acts begin? And, following on from that, what can we do to intervene?

So what exactly is the problem here?

A survey of pupil views and experiences of racism was carried out by questionnaire in two secondary schools in Hampshire (A and B) to provide a snapshot of the nature and scale of the issue. The questionnaire was completed anonymously by pupils in the hope that this would encourage a higher degree of honesty in their responses.

Pupils from the more socio-economically deprived area (school B) had much more to say on the subject and demonstrated a broader range of opinions, including some disturbing, extremist views on, for example, the issue of immigration. Taken as a whole, the majority of pupils from both schools demonstrated an understanding of racism in a very broad sense, defining it as 'being treated differently because of being in a minority group for religion, skin colour, culture or nationality' (pupil from School B). However, at an individual level, a picture of inconsistency and confusion emerged and pupils seemed to lack clarity and coherence in, and basis for, their opinions. This supports Gaine's assertion that pupils' racist views are the product of misinformation:

> ...these are not random, chance misconceptions but patterned, learned, stereotyped beliefs. [Pupils] are informed of the things they believe, but they are wrong, and their education has often failed them on all the common themes they raise because it has not challenged them or engaged with such myths in any systematic way. (Gaine, 1995)

Here, Gaine clearly highlights the central role of schools in tackling racism, a role which became a legal requirement with the introduction of the *Race Relations (Amendment) Act (2000)* which gives public authorities a statutory general duty to promote race equality (www.opsi.gov.uk/acts).

The questionnaire was intended to be a water-testing mechanism with the two schools using its findings to shape and inform their anti-racist curriculum. It began with an exploration of pupils' vocabulary.

The vocabulary of racism

Pupils were first asked to list examples of any racist vocabulary they knew in order to start to construct a picture of their understanding of racism. In school B, a total of 595 examples were cited by 117 pupils – an average of five per pupil. To make these data easier to deal with, they were categorised as follows:

References	Total
References to religion	21
References to specific nationalities	181
References to physical features (appearance of hair, eyes, nose)	11
References to culture (food, clothing)	15
References to terrorism	7
References to immigrants, refugees, asylum seekers	15
References to animals	32
References to excrement	11
References to racist organisations	3
References to skin colour	206
Other references	94
Total	**595**

Figure 8.1: Categorisation of racist vocabulary of pupils at School B

Pupils from School A cited fewer examples though, with the exception of racist organisations which they did not mention at all, their vocabulary was broadly similar to that of the pupils at School B. What this showed was that references to skin colour and nationality were the most common items in pupils' lexicons of racism.

How do pupils define racism?

The pupils were asked to explain what the term racism meant to them. The following list comprises a selection of their (verbatim) responses:

- being treated differently because of being in a minority group for religion, skin colour, culture or nationality

- offending a person's ethnic origin

- name-calling based on religion, colour...

- it's a word describing a person that is black or Chinese

- beating people up

- when someone makes comments on someone's colour, language, accent etc

- being rude or hitting any coloured person (white or black) for no reason

- treating someone differently based on race, skin colour or country of birth

- being abusive and hateful towards someone of different colour and culture

- being rude to others – calling them names

- it's where you purposely do something because someone is a different race

- racist name-calling

- discriminating against someone because of their race, religion, colour

- when a white calls a black person names like chocolate and other things

- being horrible to coloured people

- being nasty to others about the colour of their skin or the way they look or speak

- being horrible about someone's appearance and their hobbies

- an opinion about someone's appearance

- when you call a black person a racist name

- when you are nasty to foreign people

- it is discrimination towards someone with a different skin colour or ethnic background

- I think it's when someone is coloured or is a different race and someone who is a white race says something racist to them like nigga because of their race

- being rude about someone's colour or country they are from

- where someone of a different culture bullies someone as they are different

- if you say something because of their skin colour

- insulting a person's differences

- racism is where someone is unpleasant to someone when they are a different colour, from a different country or have different features

- a white person making fun of the skin of black people

- it's calling people who are black unfair names

- being prejudiced to someone because of their race

- when people feel isolated or treated differently because of their race or colour of skin

- hate crime against someone because of their origin

- one race of people thinking they are superior to another race

- someone of the opposite colour

- racism is where you offend or harass someone by using their ethnic background or colour of skin as a reason to attack them

- racism is treating someone badly because of their race

- racism is name-calling and physical abuse. If someone gets in a fight with someone from another race over something not racist, the school ends up saying it is racist

- it means the hatred of someone else who is different to another person because of their colour, race or religion which can lead to harmful action

- somebody being judged because of their skin, ethnic background or religion

These responses were diverse but a number of common themes emerged, with the concept of difference playing a key role:

- differences in skin colour, nationality, religious belief/practice, culture, voice/accent, hair, race
- inequality
- physical, mental and/or verbal attacks on people because of their origins
- prejudice
- discrimination
- treating others differently
- intimidation

It can also be seen that for some pupils only white-on-black racism exists while for others there is confusion about the terminology used to talk about racism. For most, racism involves verbal or physical aggression by one group of people against another, with discriminatory practices at institutional level falling entirely outside the pupils' understanding of racism.

One male Year 11 pupil wrote '[racism is] something the school doesn't care about'.

What is happening in schools?

Here, in their own words, are pupils' examples of racist behaviours which, they say, take place at school:

Physical

- getting beaten up
- physical abuse
- fighting
- being dragged around the playground by your bag
- throwing food at coloured people
- people getting beaten up because of their skin colour

- jumping away from students as if they are dirty
- tripping people up because they are different

Verbal

- continual name-calling
- swearing
- making fun of people because of the way they look
- verbal abuse
- taking the mick
- always talking about curry
- imitating accents
- being asked how to say swear words in other languages
- insulting people
- saying people don't belong to the same school because they are a different race

General/other

- stereotyping ethnic or coloured people
- leaving someone out because they are a different race
- not sitting next to someone because they are a different colour or from a different country
- ostracism
- teachers giving coloured people the benefit of the doubt so they're not seen to be racist
- discriminating against people
- not letting someone into a friendship group because of skin colour
- gangs, ganging up
- constant picking on

Most of these behaviours are carefully and deliberately hidden from staff. Of particular concern is the suggestion that some pupils perceive some members of staff to act in biased ways when dealing with incidents. This implies a lack of trust on the part of the pupils and possibly a lack of consistency on the part of the staff when dealing with incidents.

What happens following incidents of racist name-calling?

Broadly speaking, incidents of racist name-calling in both schools were more common amongst boys than girls and in year groups 8 and 9, according to the questionnaire respondents. Over half of the pupils said that in response to such incidents they had taken no action. The main reason given for this was fear: pupils expressed concerns about getting hurt themselves or feeling threatened or intimidated by the perpetrators. Relatively few incidents were reported to teachers and one reason given for this was that pupils thought teachers would either do nothing about it or would act in biased ways. One pupil said that their response to an incident was to join in with the racist name-calling.

In the case of the isolated bilingual learner facing racist abuse, the difficulties of reporting are compounded by language barriers and by their status as the newcomer. Comments along the lines of 'there was not a problem with racism at this school before they came' illustrate the way newly arrived pupils can unwittingly attract the blame for the racism which emerges following their arrival.

Awareness of school procedures/race equality policy

Responses to these questions showed that in School A 85 per cent and in School B, 78 per cent of pupils did not know what school procedures existed – if any – for dealing with reported racist incidents. One pupil (School A) commented that his school's procedure was to 'do nothing'.

Similarly, the vast majority of pupils in both schools (90% and 87% respectively) were not aware of the existence of their school's Race Equality Policy.

How effectively schools deal with racist incidents

This question used a 1-5 grading scale and yielded similar results in both schools with the majority of pupils opting for the "neither well nor badly" middle ground and relatively few choosing the two extremes ('very well' or 'very badly').

98

Very well	well	Neither well nor badly	Not very well	Very badly
1	2	3	4	5

A few pupils chose to write additional comments relating to this question:

- it only seems to work one way. If I was racially offended, nothing is done

- we hardly get real racism

- in some cases it does, in some it doesn't [deal effectively]

- I don't know if there has been an incident that the school has dealt with

- I'm not sure 'cause I haven't been involved in anything but I think they probably do it quite effectively

- sometimes it's not taken seriously

One pupil (School A) wrote '[The school] doesn't [deal with racist incidents]'.

Pupils' understanding of the term racism

After the initial focus on pupils' first-hand experiences of racism, this question aimed to establish the breadth of pupils' understanding of the term racism itself.

- I do not condone racism in any way, shape or form especially as my mother married an Indian, speaks Hindi to a reasonable standard and had two mixed-race children

- people seem to always think it's just black people that are victims of racism but it happens to white people too but nobody seems to care

- people don't realise racism works against white people as well

- I think that racism is wrong and should never be used against anyone in any way. People may find it fun to do to others but they probably don't realise how much it hurts mostly emotionally but

99

sometimes physically and could seriously scare them. People that are racist might like it and think it's fun but they wouldn't like being called it themselves and should stop

- people don't always report racism. Some people get bullied but don't want to say anything

- it's not just white versus black. Black versus black and black versus white also. Racist names have become just nicknames

- in an incident mentioned earlier, the coloured people were being racist to my friends and provoking racist remarks knowing that the police would be on their side

- lots of people are racist in secret and do not believe they are racist

- racism doesn't only affect coloured people. White people also have racist attacks but it is more likely that it is a coloured person. Some people are racists because they don't understand

- racism I don't think is a problem in this school

- our school isn't that racist (x2)

- I believe that everyone should be treated the same and equally

- I don't see that much racism around school

- it's horrible

- I think racism is horrible

- I think racism is not nice. So don't be racist

- it shouldn't matter what colour you are, it's the person inside you

- racism is horrible and anyone who says racism [makes racist comments] should be fined or shot. It's out of order

- for some reason, if a white person suffered from racial abuse, nothing is done but if a white person does it back, he gets arrested!

Other comments

The final question gave pupils an opportunity to make any other comments or observations they wished.

Comments pupils made about their school:

- I would like our school to be much stricter about bullying

- I think the school should make it clear what the procedures are for racial abuse and how they deal with it

- the school needs to take non-racist abuse into account before making out the fight started because of racist abuse

More general comments (all School B):

- I am 100% against immigration. Send the immigrants back – they leech off the country

- there is too much immigration

- they deserve it if they come over here and steal our jobs and our tax money and they have the nerve to insult our country. DEPORT THEM!

- there are some black people that fulfil the racist stereotype and that try to change our country and they encourage the stereotypes

- I don't agree with it but it has become more recognised in society and it is hard not to be racist at all, even when not around people who it may be aimed at

Key messages emerging from the data

From the questionnaire analyses, it would seem that racism, especially racist name-calling is commonplace in both schools – in fact far more common than the schools' annual returns to county would suggest – and this is reflected in county data which show racist name-calling far outstripping other categories of racist incidents. Pupils can cite a wide range of examples of racist vocabulary and their definitions of what might constitute racism are similarly broad and varied. However, what also emerged was a picture of inconsistency and confusion, reflecting the 'learned misinformation' referred to by Gaine (2005).

Pupil comments suggest there is a developing problem with the relationship between members of the different ethnic groups currently attending school B in particular. This seems to relate specifically to pupils originating from Nepal, the largest ethnic group on roll after white British.

Language differences also seem to be divisive: the Nepali pupils share a common language whereas pupils who might describe themselves as black (black British, black African, black other, black Caribbean etc) often speak English. Other cultural and linguistic groups are represented by only one or two isolated pupils and so may be less threatening in the eyes of the majority, possibly because they are less used and therefore less heard around the school. Some pupils, in their responses to the question-naire, made specific reference to language differences, indicating mis-trust.

Responses given by pupils at both schools suggest they often feel power-less to take action against racist incidents. Some say they want their school to take a more proactive role, to clearly explain procedures – and then follow them. There seems to be a real need for the schools to act on this feedback.

There is a suggestion that some pupils think that staff – and police – act in a biased way when dealing with a racist incident. Pupils also suggest staff sometimes label an incident as racist when their own perception is that it was not racially motivated. This indicates a possible need for staff support and training in order to achieve a shared understanding of racism and greater consistency and confidence in their approach to dealing with reported racist incidents. It would be useful to ensure that pupils were also given opportunities to develop their own understanding of racism and to consider ways in which they might become more actively involved in school procedures.

Pupils are generally not aware of the schools' Race Equality Policies. As these policies are meant to be there for them as well as to fulfil the require-ments of the Race Relations (Amendment) Act (2000), it might be advis-able to seek ways of encouraging their involvement in policy develop-ment and implementation.

What could have happened next

The whole research exercise would be pointless were it not to lead to fundamental changes in approach and ethos at the participating schools. The findings suggest a number of areas for development which may be worth further exploration.

Consideration could be given to how pupils might be given opportunities to be involved with the on-going development of the school's race equality policy/action plans. This might begin with a drive to raise awareness of procedures for dealing with racist incidents through assembly, lunchtime clubs, Personal Health and Social Education (PHSE) or tutor time.

Staff may need training in anti-racist strategies to make sure that everyone is sufficiently confident to recognise and deal with a racist incident in a consistent manner. An audit of staff views might help establish the level of need. Pupils also need opportunities to develop their own understanding of racism in its many guises through discussion and focused activities.

An assessment of the relevance of the current curriculum to the school's pupils might reveal areas for development. It may be possible to increase the school's intercultural curriculum through, for example, food technology. If pupils had more direct experience of Asian cuisine, they might be less prone to making racist remarks such as 'curry muncher'. Black History Month (October) would provide further opportunities to widen pupils' experiences, though these should be reinforced throughout the academic year.

The stock of books in the school library should include works by authors from a range of cultural backgrounds with the non-fiction stock being similarly representative of diverse cultures. Resources used by teachers should also represent other cultural traditions.

Raising the profile of other languages spoken by pupils attending the school would provide an opportunity to boost the confidence of pupils with EAL and raise their status. Some schools include willing/able bilingual pupils on a list of in-house interpreters who are called on if there are visitors to the school who speak their language. Others have a buddying scheme in operation for newly arrived pupils whereby pupils are paired with a buddy who shares the same home language. This could be developed and formalised. The use of other languages on display boards would be another opportunity that could easily be exploited. The school library could also arrange to borrow books in other languages while leaflets and DCSF information in other languages could be made available in the reception area to start to take the needs of parents into account.

What actually happened next

In school A, a member of senior management did a tour of tutor groups explaining the school's procedures for dealing with racist incidents to each. Some work was done by pupils in Year 9 on the holocaust and a display was put up in one of the main corridors. An evening for the parents of Nepali pupils was held with an interpreter present. The head talked about school rules and regulations but did not offer any opportunity for parents to ask questions or raise issues.

In school B, pupils in Year 7 received similar input on school procedures from a member of senior management. A buddying system was set up pairing existing pupils with new arrivals and matching languages where possible. A section on racist bullying was added to the school's anti-bullying leaflet, available to all pupils in the school library – in English only. A social evening was held for the parents of Nepali pupils to come and meet school staff and further meetings are planned for them to meet some of the other parents. Non-Nepali parents continue to be excluded from such events, marginalising them and their children's needs still further.

In neither school did any staff training take place after the research was shared. Nor were any significant changes to the curriculum made. The library stock and other resources used in school were not audited or updated and there was no increase in pupil involvement in school procedures. These measures could be addressed in the future as part of the on-going development of schools' anti racist approaches.

At school A in 2007, a parent wrote to express concern at the growing number of pupils from minority ethnic backgrounds admitted and the adverse affect this would have on their own children's education. School staff began to express concern at the lack of integration as numbers of pupils with English as an additional language continued to increase. At school B, the number of racist incidents continued to climb over the following two years with the need for police involvement also increasing. Pupils continued not to report incidents until matters had got out of hand. One member of staff reported, off the record, their concerns with the way other teachers referred to pupils from minority ethnic backgrounds during staff briefings.

There is most definitely still a problem here. We are not all white, thanks – much work remains to be done.

What could you do in your own school?

Carrying out a questionnaire is time-consuming and requires careful planning. Before using a questionnaire, it is advisable to consider the type of data you want to collect and how these might be handled. My questionnaire yielded a lot of soft data which do not readily lend themselves to collation or provide bases for hard statistical analysis. Furthermore, after many hours' sifting through the completed questionnaire papers, it was possible only to arrive at what Bassey terms 'fuzzy generalisations' (Bassey, 1999) rather than 'concrete, universal truths'. I was also aware of the possibility that my questionnaire might be inaccessible to pupils with limited English – although to provide written translations of the questions into the range of languages required would be expensive and would sacrifice pupil anonymity. It would, however, be very useful to find a way of collecting the views of such pupils, perhaps using interpreters who could translate the questions orally and then record pupils' responses in English on the questionnaire paper. Some useful tips on questionnaire design can be found in Cohen, Manion and Morrison's book, *Research Methods in Education* (2000), while a copy of the questionnaire I used can be found in Appendix 1. It may provide a useful starting point, should you want to carry out a similar exercise in your own setting.

Having said this, I believe that the exercise provided a useful and detailed picture of pupils' experiences and understanding of racism and pointed a spotlight on areas which the schools needed to address. However, I found that neither school seemed to take the findings particularly seriously and their follow-up actions did not constitute coherent, planned approaches to tackling racist attitudes supported by key members of the senior management team. Instead, they were piecemeal, one offs which barely scratched the surface of the underlying problem. For some practical guidance on addressing racism at institutional level and with staff and pupils, see Dadzie's *Toolkit for Tackling Racism in Schools* (2000). This should help ensure you achieve greater effectiveness in your school's approach to dealing with the issue.

One key message which emerged from my research was that pupils felt very strongly about issues to do with racism and this indicates that quality work in this area would be likely to be a rich and productive educational experience for all involved. To make sure you capitalise on this, I would recommend you:

- ensure such an approach had the full backing of the head and members of the senior management team and that they were committed to following up your work

- ensure your proposed research was included in your school's Action Plan for race equality or equivalent documentation to support your school's Race Equality Policy

- enlist the support of colleagues who might help with the collation of data

- accept that you may encounter resistance from some staff members and/or highlight staff training needs

- be prepared for pupils' responses to shock

Sarah Coles has worked with ethnic minority students in Hampshire schools since 1999 as a specialist teacher adviser. Her work in secondary schools has focused on raising pupil achievement and as part of this she has undertaken small-scale surveys into pupils' experiences of racism.

Appendix 1
The questionnaire on racism

We want you to feel you can be honest with your comments so all answers will be treated in strictest confidence. You do not have to give your name.

1. What racist words do you know/have you heard people using? Please list as many of them as you can remember. Don't worry about spelling.

2. Have you ever been called a name you consider to be racist?   Yes   No

   a. If yes, what was it (please state)?

   b. What did you do about it?

   c. If you took no action, why not?

   d. If you reported it, what action was taken?

   e. Were you happy with the outcome?   Yes   No

3. Have you ever heard anyone else calling someone a racist
   name?   Yes   No

   a. If yes, did you do anything about it? Yes No

   b. What did you do?

   c. If no, why not (what stopped you)?

   d. What was the outcome?

4. Have you ever called someone a racist name?   Yes   No

   a. If yes, what did you say?

   b. If yes, why (what was going on at the time)?

   c. Did anything happen as a result? If so, what?

5. Please list any other examples of racist behaviour that have taken place at your school.

6. Do you know what procedures your school follows when a racist incident is reported?   Yes   No

7. Do you know if your school has a Race Equality Policy?   Yes   No

8. How well do you think your school deals with racism/racist incidents?

Very well	well	Neither well nor badly	Not very well	Very badly
1	2	3	4	5

9. What does the word 'racism' mean to you?

10. Please use the rest of this page to note any other comments you have.

Glossary

BA	Bilingual Assistant
BESD	Behavioural, Emotional and Social Difficulties
BNP	British National Party
BSL	British Sign Language
CAF	Common Assessment Framework
CPE	Certificate of Primary Education
CSE	Certificate in Secondary Education
CYP	Children and Young People
DCSF	Department for Children, Schools and Families
DES	Department for Education and Science
DfES	Department for Education and Skills
EAL	English as an Additional Language
EFL	English as a Foreign Language
EM	Ethnic Minority
EMA	Ethnic Minority Achievement
EMLD	Ethnic Minority Learning Disability project
EP	Educational Psychologist
ESOL	English for Speakers of Other Languages
HI	Hearing Impairment
HLTA	Higher Level Teaching Assistant
IELTS	International English Language Testing System
LA	Local Authority

MLD   Moderate Learning Difficulties

MSI   Multi-sensory Impairment

NARIC   National Recognition Information Centre

NC   National Curriculum

NVQ   National Vocational Qualification

OCN   Open College Network

OfSTED   Office for Standards in Education

OPSI   Office of Public Sector Information

PD   Physical Disabilities

PHSE   Personal, Health and Social Education

QCA   Qualifications and Curriculum Authority

SEAL   Supporting English as an Additional Language

SEAL   Social and Emotional Aspects of Learning

SEF   Self Evaluation Form

SEN   Special Educational Needs

SIP   School Improvement Partner

SLCN   Speech, Language and Communication Needs

SpLD   Specific Learning Difficulties

TA   Teaching Assistant

TEAL   Teaching English as an Additional Language

UCSA   Unaccompanied Children Seeking Asylum

VI   Visual Impairment

References

Alladina, S (1995) *Being Bilingual: a guide for parents, teachers and young people on mother tongue heritage language and bilingual education.* Stoke on Trent: Trentham

Bassey, M (1999) *Case Study Research in Educational Settings.* Buckingham: Open University Press

Betancourt, J, Green, A, and Carillo, J (2002) *Cultural Competence in Health Care: emerging frameworks and practical approaches.* London: The Commonwealth Fund

Bignall, T and Butt, J (2000) *Between Ambition and Achievement: young black distressed people's views and experiences of independence and independent living.* Bristol: Policy Press/ JRF

Blatchford, I (1994) *The Early Years: laying the foundations for racial equality.* Stoke-on-Trent: Trentham

Bourne, J (1989) *Moving into the Mainstream: LEA provision for bilingual pupils.* Windsor: NFER-Nelson

Cline, T, De Abreu, G, Fihosy, C, Gray, H, Lambert, H and Neale, J (2002) *Minority Ethnic Pupils in Mainly White Schools.* London:DfES.

Cohen, L, Manion, L and Morrison, K (2000) *Research Methods in Education (Fifth Edition).* London and New York: RoutledgeFalmer

Cooke, S and Pike, S (2000) *Developing language-aware teaching in secondary schools.*

CVS consultants (2004) Learning Disabilities and BME communities in Hampshire: final report. Unpublished document, CVS consultants

Dadzie, S (2000) *Toolkit for Tackling Racism in Schools.* Stoke-on-Trent: Trentham

DES (1985) *Education For All (The Swann Report).* London: HMSO

DfES (2000) *Secondary National Strategy (formerly KS3 strategy).* London: HMSO

DfES (2001) *The SEN Code of Practice.* London: HMSO

DfES (2002a) *Access and Engagement in History: teaching pupils for whom English is an additional language. Key Stage 3, National Strategy.* London: DfES ref: 0656/2002

DfES (2002b) *Teaching Assistant File: induction training for teaching assistants in primary/ secondary schools. EAL module.* London: DfES

DfES (2003) *Materials for School – involving parents, raising achievement.* London: HMSO.

DfES (2004a) *English as an Additional Language: induction training for teaching assistants in primary and secondary schools.* London: HMSO

DfES (2004b) *Every Child Matters: change for children.* London: HMSO

DfES (2004c) *Special Educational Needs and Disability Update 16.* London: HMSO

DfES (2005a) *Aiming High: guidance on the assessment of pupils learning English as an additional language.* London: HMSO

DfES (2005b) *Marking Progress: training materials for assessing English as an additional language.* London: HMSO

DfES (2006) *Excellence and Enjoyment: learning and teaching for bilingual children in the primary years.* London: HMSO

DfES and DCSF (2007) *New Arrivals Excellence Programme. Guidance.* London: DfES

DfES and Ofsted (2004) *New Relationship with Schools.* London: DfES

Department of Health (2001) *Valuing People: a new strategy for learning disability for the 21st century.* London: Department of Health Publications

Flouri, E and Buchanan, A (2004) Early father's and mother's involvement and child's later educational outcomes. *British Journal of Educational Psychology* 74, p141-153

Franson, C (1999) Mainstreaming learners of English as an additional language: the class teacher's perspective. *Language, Culture and Curriculum* 12 (1)

Gaine, C (1987) *No Problem Here: a practical approach to education and 'race' in white schools.* London: Hutchison

Gaine, C (1995) *Still No Problem Here.* Stoke-on-Trent: Trentham

Gaine, C (2005) *We're All White, Thanks.* Stoke-on-Trent: Trentham

Gibbons, P C (1993) Learning to Learn in a Second Language. Portsmouth: Heinemann

Gravelle, M (2000) *Planning for Bilingual Learners: an inclusive curriculum.* Stoke-on-Trent: Trentham

Hall, D (1995) *Assessing the Needs of Bilingual Pupils: living in two languages.* London: David Fulton

Hampshire County Council (2005) *Change for Children Programme.* Winchester: Hampshire County Council

Hampshire County Council (2006) *Children and Young People's Plan.* Winchester: Hampshire County Council

Home Office (2000) *Race Relations Amendment Act.* London: Home Office

Husain, F (2005) *Cultural competence in family support.* London: National Family and Parenting Institute

Kenner, C (2000) *Home Pages: literacy links for bilingual children.* Stoke-on-Trent : Trentham

Leung, C (2007) English as an Additional Language Policy: issues of inclusive access and language learning in the mainstream. *Naldic Quarterly* 4 (3) p16-24

Lindsay, G, Pather, S and Strand, S (2006) *Special Educational Needs and Ethnicity: issues of over-and under-representation.* London: DfES

McKee, D (1989) *Elmer.* London: Random House

Mir, G and Din, I (2003) *Communication, Knowledge and Chronic Illness in the Pakistani Community.* Leeds: Centre for research in primary care, University of Leeds

Mir, G, and Tovey, P (2002) Cultural Competency: professional action and South Asian carers. *Journal of Management in Medicine.* 16 (1) p 7-19

Office for Public Management (2006) Valuing People and Ethnic Minority Communities: report for Hampshire learning disability partnership board. Unpublished document, Office for Public Management

Ofsted (2001) *Inspecting English as an Additional Language.* London: HMSO

QCA (2000) *A Language in Common: assessing English as an additional language.* London: QCA

Rosamond, S, Bhatti, I, Sharieff, M and Wilson K (2003) *Distinguishing the Difference SEN or EAL?* Birmingham: Birmingham Advisory and Support Service

Shields, C (2002) *Unless.* London and Glasgow: Fourth Estate

Statham, E (1993) Scattered in the mainstream: educational provision for isolated bilingual learners. Unpublished PhD thesis, University of Southampton

Stanton, J (1999) Induction of newly arrived, older bilingual pupils in schools. *Language Issues* 11 (1)

Thomas, W and Collier, V (1997) *School Effectiveness for Language Minority Students.* Washington DC: National Clearing House for Bilingual Education

Valuing People Support Team (nd) Improving Services for People with Learning Disabilities from Minority Ethnic Groups: report to the learning disability taskforce with recommendations for a report to the minister. Unpublished document, Valuing People Support team

Virgo, L (2006) *Reaching Out.* London: Mencap

Wardak, A (2007) Focused Implementation Site for Delivering Race Equality in Mental Health Care, *Newsletter*, 6

Wong Fillmore, L (1980) Learning a Second Language: Chinese children in the American class-room. In Alatis J (ed) *Georgetown University Round Table on Language and Linguistics.* Washington DC: Georgetown University Press

Resources

www3.hants.gov.uk/education/hias/intercultural/intercultural-raceequality

www.hants.gov.uk/education/ema

www.hants.gov.uk/museum

www.mantralingua.com

www.opsi.gov.uk/acts

www.speakeasyadvocacy.org.uk/about

Ruth Hayman Trust PO Box 17685 London N6 6WD

Index